George W. Quinby

Heaven Our Home

The Christian doctrine of the resurrection: showing man the victor over sin and

death

George W. Quinby

Heaven Our Home

The Christian doctrine of the resurrection: showing man the victor over sin and death

ISBN/EAN: 9783337403232

Printed in Europe, USA, Canada, Australia, Japan

Cover: Foto ©Lupo / pixelio.de

More available books at **www.hansebooks.com**

HEAVEN OUR HOME:

The Christian Doctrine of the Resurrection;

SHOWING

Man the Victor over Sin and Death.

A COMFORT TO ALL WHO MOURN AND A HELP TO SUCH AS
NEED FAITH IN GOD AND HOPE OF HEAVEN.

BY REV. G. W. QUINBY, D. D.

"We are conquerors and more than conquerors through Him that loved us."—PAUL.
"Blessed are they that mourn for they shall be comforted."—CHRIST.

SEVENTH EDITION.

AUGUSTA, ME.:
GOSPEL BANNER OFFICE.
1882.

Copyrighted
BY GEORGE W. QUINBY,
1876.

TO

THE MEMORY OF

THOSE

NEAR AND DEAR TO THE AUTHOR,

NOW IN

THEIR BEAUTIFUL HOME ABOVE,

THIS VOLUME

IS AFFECTIONATELY INSCRIBED.

Heaven our Home.

We are but strangers here,
  Heaven is our home;
Earth has its gath'ring cheer,
  But Heaven is our home:
Danger and sorrow stand
Round us on every hand;
Heaven is our fatherland,—
  Heaven is our home.

What though the tempest rage,
  Heaven is our home;
Short is our pilgrimage,
  Heaven is our home:
Time's cold and wintry blast
Soon will be overpast;
We shall reach home at last;
  Heaven is our home.

There, at our Saviour's side,
  Heaven is our home;
We shall be glorified,
  Heaven is our home:
There are the millions blest,
Those we loved most and best,
And there we, too, shall rest;
  Heaven is our home!

PREFACE.

This volume is sent forth from the heart of its author in the earnest hope that it will add joy to other hearts. There are clouds and tears enough;—we would bring sunshine and smiles. Great errors exist concerning Death and the Future, —errors that are the cause of very much sorrow in the world. Millions are in sadness because of their belief that there is no hereafter but that death is the end of all that is beautiful and noble which they love. Other millions mourn because of the more shocking belief that they themselves, or the dear objects of their affection, will be made to suffer long ages in a purgatorial condition of banishment from God, or endlessly after death, and all because of the nature God has given them in this life. And other millions still, weep simply because cherished ones have been removed from their embrace, and they are left alone in the world. For the hands and hearts of all such this volume is specially designed. By the proofs it contains of the certainty of another and more joyful existence for every soul of God's great family in Heaven at last, it would comfort all that are sad, giving them the oil of joy for mourning, the garment of praise for the spirit of heaviness, and reconciling them to the Providence of that Infinite Being who is too wise to err and too good to be unkind.

That this result may be happily realized by those for whom the book is designed, is the warm prayer of

THE AUTHOR.

Augusta, Me., June 1, 1876.

CONTENTS.

CHAPTER I.
Preliminary Reflections.

Practice of the Author as Editor.—Kind requests for an Expression of his Views on the Resurrection and Kindred Subjects.—Letters Received.—Interest felt on the General Subject.—Vagueness which exists concerning it.—Need of Correct Views.—The Author's thoughts presented in no Spirit of Dogmatism. - - - - 11

CHAPTER II.
"If a Man Die shall he Live Again?"

"To be, or not to be, that's the Question."—The Nature of our Existence.—Man's thoughts in the Contemplation of Death.—The Desire to Live innate in Man.—All our Inborn Longings are gratified.—God cannot deny Himself. - - - - - - 21

CHAPTER III.
"If a Man Die shall he Live Again?"

Every creature follows its own Instincts.—Instinct never craves what does not exist.—Illustrations.—The inherent desire of Man for Another Life, and yet Man possesses no indwelling desire for what is not.—The aged Unbeliever.—His Conversion through the presence of ministering angels.—The ecstacy of his joy as he neared the River of Death which he found spanned with the bow of promise. - 32

CHAPTER IV.
What is the Resurrection? How and when shall it Transpire?

The common Views.—Unbelief of Paul.—His strong Faith after His conversion.—Distinction between the Man and the House he Lives in.—Luminous Views of Paul.—Great and Beautiful Truth perfectly answering the spiritual needs of the soul. - - - 40

CHAPTER V.
The Resurrection in Harmony with Nature.

Paul's reasoning with Agrippa who denied the doctrine of the Resurrection.—What is there in this doctrine more difficult to comprehend or harder to belive than many other things in Nature.—The Resurrection not against Nature, but in harmony with it.—Wonderful transformation of the Worm into the Butterfly.—The Resurrection a Birth of the Soul into Another Life.—Shall we retain consciousness during the process of the Resurrection? - - - - - 50

CONTENTS.

CHAPTER VI.

Doctrine of the Resurrection Strengthened by a Further Appeal to Nature.

Men will believe in the Truths of Nature and yet deny the truths of their own nature.—Facts in the Natural World.—Laws which govern the Spiritual do certainly exist.—Change in the Body.—Change in the Soul.—Wonders in the Visible World.—Why not Wonders in the Spiritual World? - - - - - - - - 63

CHAPTER VII.

The Death of the Body no Proof of the Destruction of the Soul.

Nothing in Nature is ever absolutely Destroyed.—Changes by Fire, Flood, Death and universal Decomposition are continually taking place, but change never necessarily implies Destruction.—Vegetation is constantly springing into Existence and falling to Decay, but not a particle of its Substance is lost.—Nor is it possible to destroy the inward Forces which control matter.—If, then, the absolute Destruction of the Body is Impossible, is it probable the divine Essence of the Soul Perishes?—Facts adduced. - - - - - 75

CHAPTER VII.

The Soul's Triumph over the Body.

The main argument of the Materialist considered.—No man knows or can prove that the Soul Perishes on the Death and Dissolution of the Body.—Thousands have testified that they have seen and conversed with their Departed Friends.—Interesting Facts.—Testimony of Medical Men.—Dr. Kane's assertion.—Apparent Death of a Clergyman.—What he Saw and Heard.—Interesting Facts.—The Soul's Triumph over the Body in Death. - - - - - - 83

CHAPTER IX.

The Question of No Moral Change by a Change of Worlds, considered.

The Errors that Prevail in the Church relative to the Resurrection.—If the common Notions are Correct, Heaven can be a place of Happiness to None.—Modified Views of Restorationists and some Universalists not Sustained by the New Testament.—Consideration of the Question, Is there any Moral Change in Man in consequence of a change of Worlds?—Interesting Facts stated. - - - 107

CHAPTER X.

What is the Nature of the Change Wrought by a Change of Worlds.

A Change of Worlds Necessitates a Change of Bodies.—Plain Teaching of the Apostle on this Subject.—Imperfection and Sinful Nature of our Physical Bodies.—The Glory, Perfection and Wondrous Beauty of our Celestial Bodies. - - - - - - 121

CHAPTER XI.

A Change of Bodies not the only Change Man Experiences by a Change of Worlds.

Difference between the Terrestrial and Celestial Body.—The Purity and Glory of the Latter.—Can this Radical Change take place with Man and not affect him as a Moral Being?—Can a sinful Soul occupy a sinless Body? - - - - - - - 132

CHAPTER XII.

Elevating and Renovating Power of the Resurrection.

The Scriptural Usage of the Word Anastasis, translated Resurrection.—It is sometimes applied to Man's Moral and Spiritual Up-rising.—Its meaning as Employed by the Apostle in describing Man's Birth into the Other Life.—Out of the Mortal into the Immortal.—Out of the Earthly into the Heavenly.—The Glory of the Future Life when compared with this. - - - - - - - 141

CHAPTER XIII.

Excellence and Perfection of our Future Bodies.

The Soul.—Sin, how does it Originate?—The Spiritual Body not only Beautiful but Perfect.—Hence, no such mistakes as Sin are made in the Future.—The Spiritual Brain.—Wonderful Powers of the Soul when in a Mesmeric Trance.—What may not be its possibilities in the Resurrection Life when relieved of the Clogs of the Flesh?—The Cape Ann Clairvoyant Boy.—The Somnambulist and of what he is capable. - - - - - - - 150

CHAPTER XIV.

Sinless Condition of the Resurrection Life. Positive Testimony of Paul and Christ.

What we have shown concerning Man's Earthly Nature and his Heavenly Nature.—His Home on Earth and his Home in Heaven.—The Positive Teaching of the Apostle and Christ.—Man to be the Victor over Death and Sin and Pain.—The Opinions of leading Writers on this Theme. - - - - - - - 160

CHAPTER XV.

Popular Views of our Moral and Spiritual Condition Shown to be Errors.

Men say that Dying is simply throwing off one's Physical Body, like casting aside his garments, or like Passing from one Room into another.—These Ideas shown to be Errors.—The Beauty and Glory of our Future Home in Heaven when compared with our Life Here.—The Conditions of the Heavenly World all favorable to our Purity and Growth.—Beautiful Thoughts from an Eminent Writer. - 173

CHAPTER XVI.

Views of the Objector Considered.

The Objector may say that it still appears to him Men will Sin in the Other Life.—If so, what will be the Nature of the Sins he will Commit?—This Question should be Carefully Considered.—The Body the great Inciting Cause of Sin.—Hatred in the Soul not possible in the Heavenly Life.—Impossible for us to possess the same Characters in the Resurrection that we have Here. - - - - 183

CHAPTER XVII.

Christ—The Object of his Mission—Heir of all Things—The Resurrection and the Life.

If the Doctrine advanced in these Pages be true, how is Christ the Savior of Men?—The Perfect Work of the Gospel not fully accomplished in this Life.—Pre-existence of Christ.—He is Heir of all Things.—The Head of every Man.—The Resurrection and the Life.—The Savior of the World. - - - - - - - 192

CHAPTER XVIII.

Conditions of our Heavenly Home Considered and Questions Answered.

Shall all stand on an Equality in the Future Life?—Can there be Progression There?—Shall we feel accountable to God and under the same obligations to Love and Serve Him we do in this Life, and will all be equally happy There?—Infinite Diversity both Here and Hereafter.—Sublime Truths concerning Heaven. - - - 204

CHAPTER XIX.

Rewards and Punishments—Will they be Meted out in the Resurrection Life?

Why Punish a Being who is Pure and Holy and can never more Commit a Wrong?—The Doctrine of the Church not believed by the Church.—The Doctrine of Rewards—The Scriptures silent on the Subject.—What is Punishment?—It is Corrective and hence cannot be Endless. - - - - - - - - 216

CHAPTER XX.

Partial Evil and Inequality Harmonized with Infinite Goodness.

Inequalities of this World.—No two are precisely the same at Death.—How can they occupy precisely the same Conditions in the Resurrection?—Impossible to Harmonize an Endless Evil with Infinite Goodness.—Man is Imperfect but not placed wrong.—God makes no Mistakes.—Each one in the Future shall be Perfectly Happy in His Sphere. - - - - - - - 232

CHAPTER XXI.

Shall We Know Each Other in Heaven?

Those who have passed into the Higher Life can see us and they know us.—This is not the Hope of all.—Reasons for Belief in this Beautiful Truth.—If we have no knowledge of our Friends in Heaven, we shall have no knowledge of anything that existed on Earth.—Teachings of the Bible relative to the Subject.—Thoughts Sublimely Beautiful. 241

CHAPTER XXII.

Our Knowledge of Those We Love in Heaven—Objections Considered.

How can Disembodied Spirits be Seen or Known?—Spiritual Forms not only Real but Beautiful.—Methods of Knowing in Heaven not Possessed on Earth.—If we possess Knowledge of each other in Heaven shall we not have Knowledge of the sufferings of those on Earth and in the World of Misery?—And, if so, will not this Knowledge be a source of perpetual sorrow in Heaven? - - - - 253

CHAPTER XXIII.

Heaven a Home of Blessedness for All.

The Grand Consummation of the Gospel.—Why should we fear the Change called Death?—Christ and Death at the Gate of Nain.—Dr. Priestly and the Rev. John Murray when dying.—A Home in Heaven for All. - - - - - - - - 262

CHAPTER XXIV.

Letter of Condolence from Benjamin Franklin.

The Present Life Transient.—The Future Real.—The Benevolence of God plainly Exhibited in the Change called Death.—We must Surrender our Mortal Bodies for the Immortal.—Beautiful, Comforting Thought. - - - - - - - - 266

POETRY.

Shall We Know the Loved Ones There. - - - 261
When the Mists have Rolled Away We Shall Know as We are Known. - - - - - - - - 268
My Little Boy in Heaven. - - - - - - 269
To Alice Among the Angels. - - - - - 270
The Aged.—"Only Waiting." - - - - - 272

HEAVEN OUR HOME.

CHAPTER I.

Preliminary Reflections.

Practice of the Author as Editor.—Kind requests for an Expression of his Views on the Resurrection and Kindred Subjects.—Letters Received.—Interest felt on the General Subject.—Vagueness which exists concerning it.—Need of Correct Views.—The Author's thoughts presented in no Spirit of Dogmatism.

HAVING made it a practice for some years, as editor of a Christian paper, to answer the questions of correspondents concerning the teachings of the Scriptures, relative to God, Christ, sin, punishment, the judgment, heaven, hell, etc., we have recently received letters from different sources, respectfully asking our views concerning the Christian doctrine of the Resurrection,—its nature,—the relation of the Present with the Future Life,—the condition of man in the spirit world, etc., etc. Some of these communications were from Brethren in the ministry,—old and young; others from laymen, and from youth of both sexes; others from teachers in Sabbath-schools, and others still, from persons bowed down with grief in consequence of the loss of those near and dear to their hearts. These communications all appeared to breathe the spirit of sincerity and earnest inquiry. The following are samples:

A devoted and affectionate sister in Christ, writes:

"My dear mother died last week. I am greatly bereaved, as I loved her as I did myself, and even more devotedly. She and I were all in all to each other, as I was her only child, and father passed away fifteen years ago. * * * Do you believe she is now *already* risen, and in the spirit world, and happy? Can she see me and does she know how sad and lonely I feel without her?"

A much respected Brother in the ministry, in commenting on remarks of ours in a previous number of our paper, says:

"Let me inquire: What is your view definitely, of the Christian *anastasis* or the resurrection? Do you believe the resurrection takes place immediately at or after death? Do you believe that any of mankind had experienced the resurrection or had passed into the higher state that God designed for man, previous to the resurrection of Christ—previous to his ascension, etc.? Does the resurrection bring man out of a state of unconsciousness? Do you believe in the resurrection of these material bodies? Does the resurrection consist in putting on a spiritual body?"

A young Brother clergyman asks:

"Do you believe there will be any moral change in man on his passing from this life into the next? Shall we not be *sinners* there as well as here? If not, what is to prevent? Surely we shall have the same *minds* there as here."

Another still, who seemed much exercised in his mind in the general questions involved, said:

* * * "In my preaching, I hardly ever touch upon the subject of future sin and future punishment, because I am not in my own mind entirely clear on that point. * * * If we sin in the future life, as we shall if we are the same morally as we are when we die, we shall be punished; but if we possess natures that will lead us to sin in that other world, *when* will our sinning cease. and we be holy and happy? * * * If you will give your views on this subject, I shall be under great obligations. * * * Do not mention my name."

During the progress of our efforts to present our views on the above questions, an intelligent layman addressed us as follows:

"I see you are answering the queries of sundry writers relative to the nature of the resurrection and another life, but would it not be better first of all to settle the question, 'Is there another life?' With me, 'to be or not to be, *that's* the question.' A patriarch of the olden time, many years ago, asked 'If a man die, shall he live again?' *He* seemed interested in that question. It interests *me*. It is a question that no man has positively decided, and I do not think any man can positively decide it by proof; but I should be glad to see your views on this subject, as they might strengthen my faith in another existence. God knows—if there is a God —that there is nothing I so much desire as an unshaken faith in the certainty of such an existence, for then I should believe that I should not cease to exist, that my sainted mother and angel wife and our dear Nelly still live and that I shall go to them and know them, and they will know me and we should again enjoy each other's society. Indeed, all that I possess on earth I would give with the greatest pleasure, could I but feel and know in my soul that this is true!"

These are important queries involving vital interests. Their authors will please accept our thanks for the kindness of their words and the confidence their requests imply. Our only regret is lack of ability to answer them in a manner to meet their expectations and establish their faith clearly, as we could desire, in the cheering and comforting truths of the New Testament. But this would be expecting too much. We can only give our reasons for our own hope, with the prayer that these reasons may meet the needs of other souls and win them to their acceptance.

The subjects embraced are comprehensive. To discuss them with profit to the reader, several chapters will be required. These we propose to give, and we do it all the more cheerfully and with greater earnestness, for the following reasons:—

1. Because there seems to exist at the present time, a wide-spread and deep interest in the questions involved. There never was a time when persons of our own sect manifested so earnest a desire to know what the Scriptures teach on the subjects embraced in the foregoing letters, as at the present moment. Nor is this interest confined to people of our own church. We are constantly meeting with persons in social intercourse, and in our travels, of

all religious beliefs,—Congregationalists, Baptists, Methodists, Free Baptists, Unitarians and others who say the common notions of the resurrection in which they were educated, involving the unconscious condition of the soul for ages, and the re-production of these veritable bodies from their graves, in the resurrection life, many of them old, worn out, decrepit, corrupt, full of disease and horridly loathsome at the time of death, they cannot believe in; nor can they comprehend how beings purely spiritual as the New Testament represents them to be in the coming life, can be in a condition of greater depravity and wickedness and wretchedness than in this life,—and they talk as if nothing would give them more sincere delight than some reasonable, scriptural solution of this question, founded on the philosophy of nature and in harmony with the longings of their own souls. Hence, any approach we can make toward the accomplishment of this object will prove a source of joy to us.

2. We enter upon this duty the more cheerfully because of the necessity which exists in every man's nature for a clear and well defined system of belief in his very soul, on this great subject,—a belief which shall serve as a basis of hope strong and enduring, like that of the apostle, which was "sure and steadfast, as an anchor to his soul." Destitute of such a hope, how forlorn the heart in times of bereavement! At an unexpected moment, sickness comes to us, and we are prostrate and helpless; or

death enters our home where only health and joy have reigned, and suddenly snatches an angel child, or idolized sister, father, mother, husband, wife or other cherished one from our embrace. What grief is experienced! Yea, what anguish lacerates the soul! At such times, what can weigh with a strong, sweet, comforting faith in God, and hope of heaven? And how barren and utterly wretched must be that heart where no such faith exists! O, how many scenes of grief at such moments have we witnessed. Our frequent interviews with the sick at the bedside and with the afflicted over the remains of the dear departed, have afforded us knowledge with reference to that whereof we speak. If any person on earth is prepared for affliction, such as comes from the separation we describe, it is the man or woman who has, down deep in the soul, the faith and hope concerning another life, to which we refer, based on a clear understanding of the teachings and promises of God's word.

3. Then again we find another reason for the plain discussion of this subject, at the present time, in the fact that there are so many in our own denomination, as well as in all others, who seem to be utterly destitute of the great blessing to which we refer. There are clergymen, even, who have no well defined faith concerning the resurrection and what it implies. They permit themselves to believe in another existence, and this is about all. They never preach about it, or if they do, their hearers are just

as much in the dark at the conclusion of their efforts as when they began. There are thousands who call themselves Universalists, who have no distinct ideas of what death embraces, or what the resurrection is as taught in the New Testament,—or concerning the nature and condition of the future life, or what the Bible really teaches on these great questions. Their ideas on these subjects, like those of many persons of other sects, are the most vague imaginable. We think this could not, in truth, have been said of the members of the Universalist fraternity thirty years ago. The causes of the change and present vagueness to which we refer, may be attributed perhaps, to the fact, first, that many of our clergymen have come to deem the practical truths of religion of more worth than those that tell us of heaven and the dear ones living there; and so have gone to the other extreme in their pulpit efforts and have declared Christ the "Leader" and "Guide," but not Christ the "Resurrection" and the "Life!" And second, their instructions are less from the Bible, than were those of the fathers, and hence less definite as a system of Christian faith. Human speculations and philosophy often answer well as applied to many questions that agitate the public mind, but on this of *another* existence, nothing can take the place of the teachings of the New Testament. Christ came to bring life and immortality to light. His declarations and those of the apostles with reference to this question, when rightly comprehended, are clear and positive, and withal very comforting and beautiful, and though we turn to the nature of the human soul,—its powers, its aspirations, and to the philosophy of our being and of all things around us in the universe, for *confirmation of the truth of another existence,*—the sheet-anchor of our hope relative to that other and diviner life,—its nature, our condition there, and the certainty of its existence,—is what we find in the New Testament, in the life and teachings, death and resurrection of Christ, and the subsequent declarations, faith and hope of the apostles. Hence, the teachings of the New Testament will form the basis of our views, as given on these various subjects.

4. Further, the author of these remarks, in giving expression to these preliminary thoughts, wishes to say, very distinctly, in this place,—that he offers his views on the great questions presented, in no spirit of dogmatism, or with the idea in his heart of forcing his opinions upon others on the presumption that those who may differ from him are not as really entitled to our denominational name and to all the prerogatives of our church as he, or those who agree with him. It should be distinctly known that a Universalist is one who believes in the ultimate salvation of all souls from sin, error and suffering. Whatever views he may accept and hold with reference to all other questions, if he believes in this leading, fundamental sentiment, he is a Universalist. Hence, with reference to other and minor con-

siderations, relating to God's method in the salvation of the world, members of our fraternity who could not think alike, in the spirit of kindness and charity have "agreed to disagree" lest contention stir up strife and superinduce discord and division. And this is wise. Those who constitute the bulk of our denomination have come out from other sects among which great difference of opinion has prevailed relative to the doctrine of another life. It is not, therefore, expected that all Universalists do, or *can* entertain the same views relative to *how* and *when* the soul is made utterly free from the thraldom of sin and error; whether in this world or in the future. But we should not quarrel over this question or treat each other's views with contempt or derision, but rather permit each to entertain unmolested his own, honest convictions, and if he desires, express them in the spirit of charity that others may know what he believes, and of the joy he experiences as the fruit of his faith.

With these preliminaries that all may understand the motives that govern us, and the influences under which we write, we proceed to a consideration of the subjects proposed in the series of questions recorded at the commencement of this chapter, and will begin with the last mentioned—"Is there a future existence?" All the other questions proposed are predicated on the generally accepted truth of this, and, yet, no man can positively demonstrate its truth. This we shall not attempt in our present effort; and yet we trust we shall be able to present facts and reflections for the consideration of the reader of such a nature, as may, at least, confirm his faith in the great doctrine of a future life, and hence render him more hopeful and happy in contemplation of the future than he ever yet has been.

CHAPTER II.

"If a man die shall he live again?"

"To be, or not to be, that's the Question."—The Nature of our Existence.—Man's thoughts in the Contemplation of Death.—The Desire to Live innate in Man.—All our Inborn Longings are gratified.—God cannot deny Himself.

OUR correspondent says that with *him*, "To be or not to be, *that's the* question." And so it is with all thoughtful minds. The bare possibility of annihilation strikes the soul with dread, and the more protracted the span of our years, the more intense the dread, for the more we feel the shortness of life, the nearness of death, and the utter emptiness of all things earthly. We pause and reflect on our existence,—its nature, its end, and our possible destiny. We find ourselves inhabitants of this planet, in possession of a physical and intellectual organization, surrounded by ten thousand things as curious and wonderful as our own being. We eat, drink, sleep, engage in business, indulge in pleasure, and in social intercourse, think, hope, fear, love, hate, suffer and enjoy, and thus we pass on from day to day, and from year to year, in the pilgrimage of our earth existence. But the thought will come: How long shall we continue in this sphere? And when we die, shall we live again, or shall we perish forever like the brutes? We look up to the twinkling stars or glowing sun,—we gaze upon the broad green earth or the towering mountains; we consider the flowers of the field and all the beauties of this glad earth; we look into the dear faces of those we love, and we say—in our hearts, if not audibly—"Must I *die* to all this, absolutely DIE? I know that my body is mortal,—that ere the revolutions of a century shall be numbered, this material form, composed of flesh and bones, sinews and blood, and now so energized with life and health, will be a mass of unconscious dust. But how will it be with *me*,—the spiritual organism which constitutes the thinking, reasoning *man*,—will that also be forever unconscious? Will it possess no organized existence? No power of thought, no knowledge, no affection? Must I so speedily pass into eternal oblivion, while the bright sun continues to shine, the stars to twinkle, and the ocean to beat upon its rocky shores from age to age? And shall this also be true of those I love—husband, wife, children, parents, friends—all? When about to close their eyes in death, murmuring as they do so, a sweet and affectionate farewell,—is that the *last* word they will ever speak? The *last* look of recognition, the *last* moment of conscious existence of those so dear to us? Or shall they live again, perchance in a brighter and happier sphere?"

These are questions fraught with more interest and are of greater moment than all other questions.

From early childhood they come rushing into the soul making it all alive with doubt, hope and conjecture. This is the condition of mind of our correspondent. He says that of all questions, this with him is of the greatest moment. Thus has it been with all men. From the earliest ages of the world has it evolved the same intense interest. David and Solomon, Plato and Socrates were as deeply impressed with the magnitude of this subject, and as greatly exercised at the thought of death and annihilation, as are the sages and philosophers of our own time. Should they live again? Was death the door to the dark, deep pit of nonentity, or was it the hand of love which liberated the soul, that through the resurrection it might be translated to a higher and diviner existence?

We repeat, these thoughts are in the hearts of all men and all orders and nations of men. The desire for life and the dread of death are universal. Men do not ask to be permitted to live in the particular locality in which they were born, but often manifest a desire to migrate to some other State or country. To see other portions of the world, or even visit other planets and stars, if this were possible, would be a source of pleasure to them. But they must live *somewhere*; the thought of annihilation is so dreadful! And this feeling is not only *universal*, but it is *natural* with the soul; just as really so to a healthful soul as hunger is to a healthful body. Will our correspondent be pleased carefully to mark this fact:

—that his ardent desire for another existence is instinctive or innate in him. These are feelings which never originate outside of ourselves; they are of God, belong to the soul and their very existence is of itself strong proof of a hereafter. He says:— "God knows—if there is a God—that there is nothing I so much desire as an unshaken faith in the certainty of another life, for then I should believe that I should not cease to exist, that my sainted mother and angel wife and our dear Nelly still live and that I shall go to them and know them, and they will know me and we shall again enjoy each other's society. Indeed, all that I possess on earth I would give with the greatest pleasure, could I but feel and know in my soul that this is all true!"

How earnest these expressions. They are the outgushings of a full soul, and show that the desire for another life for himself and those dear to him is stronger than all other desires combined. All he possesses on earth, he would surrender most willingly, he says, to feel and know that he and his will live again.

These are his feelings. *How came he in possession of them?* Did he ever ask himself this question? Let him inquire of others and he will find that all his neighbors and acquaintances are in possession of similar desires, more or less intense. *How came they in possession of these desires?* There can be but one answer to this question. *As they are innate in the soul, interwoven in the very texture of our being, they must have been placed there by the great and good Being who made us,* and WHO NEVER GAVE EXISTENCE TO A DESIRE OR WANT IN THE NATURE OF ANY LIVING BEING OR CREATURE WHICH HE DID NOT GRATIFY BY THE CREATION AND BESTOWMENT OF PRECISELY THE THING NECESSARY TO ANSWER PERFECTLY THE DEMANDS OF THAT DESIRE OR WANT.

We have emphasized these words in order to impress the wonderful truth they contain upon the minds of our correspondent and all other readers, for upon this fact we found our first, great reason for a confident belief in the blessed truth that if a man die he shall live again. God Himself has placed this need in the soul. He has made it a part of our being. So He affirms through the words of the Apostle who represents man as "groaning in this tabernacle of clay, earnestly desiring to be clothed upon" with divine and heavenly garments, and enter "the building of God, the house not made with hands," which he says "we *know* is eternal in the heavens." "Now," says he, "He that hath wrought [or made] us for this self-same purpose, and given us this earnest desire, *is God.*" Do we believe this? and would God create this strongest of all desires in the souls of His sentient creatures, involving interests more vital than all others, and then mock it forever with the cold echoes of annihilation, when He kindly gratifies all other wants which He has created, however trivial?

Look at the facts, and consider. Every *living* thing to which God has given existence, has *needs*. The trees, grass, flowers, shrubbery, the corn, the grain, and indeed every species of vegetation that springs from the earth, that has life in it, has wants which must be supplied or death is inevitable. They need the healthful nourishment that comes from the dews and rains of heaven,—from the invigorating atmosphere and the bright, blessed sunshine. And the very elements vegetation craves, for health and growth and beauty, God has provided in the largest abundance in all parts of this wonderful domain.

So of all animal life. The fishes of the sea, the birds of the forests, the animals and insects that people the earth and the atmosphere, all are created with distinct wants; and these wants must be supplied or their lives would fade away and universal extinction would be the result. Now, careful examination into the facts will convince the reader that not the smallest need of the most minute insect God has made, is left unprovided for, but, on the contrary, every want is fully answered by the creation and bestowment of the very things necessary to supply those wants. O, how does this wonderful truth demonstrate to us the goodness of God—the God of the Bible,—which declares that "He openeth His hand and satisfieth the desires of every living thing."

And this is as true of man as of all else that God has made, notwithstanding man's needs are greater than those of all other creatures. His wants are not alone physical, but intellectual, moral, spiritual. The needs of the ox grazing on the lawn in the blessed summer-time are few. He crops his grassy food and drinks from the babbling brook or gushing fountain, and increases day by day in growth and vigor and beauty. How simple! But simple as it is, the want to which we refer must be supplied; and it *is* supplied precisely as it is needed, which shows how wonderful and benevolent are the providences of that great Being who would have the very beasts healthful and happy!

When we consider the nature of man, how much more numerous and diversified do we find his physical needs. How much more extended the variety of food his appetite craves; but extended as it is, every want is bountifully provided for. God creates no bodily hunger that he does not appease by furnishing some suitable reality corresponding with the want demanded. It is said that among the various nations and tribes of men on our globe, no less than six thousand different articles of food are employed for the wants and gratification of the human palate. And the physical demands of man do not end even here. Think of how abundant the supply of material from which is furnished clothing to protect and beautify the persons of a billion of God's great family, and houses and homes for their safety, accommodation and blessing. All this God has done to answer the physical wants of His sentient creatures.

We have been thus particular in our reflections, in order to impress the mind of the reader with the truth of the conclusion to which we must come, with reference to the higher and diviner needs of the soul, and the certainty that God has implanted no inherent and permanent desire in the spiritual of man's nature, for the gratification of which he has made no provision. If God has done this in any one instance it would be an exhibition of wantonness and mockery which would be utterly inconsistent with the infinite goodness of that great Being. We cannot tell what the soul is. We only feel that its essence is more divine than any thing that belongs to mere physical life. But we know *what its needs are;*—that they are intellectual, moral, spiritual. The soul craves knowledge; it loves the beautiful; it delights in music and poetry, in art, science and business. It revels in friendship, in the delights of travel and amusement, and in ten thousand other things which it enjoys, and destitute of which its happiness would be marred. *Now in every single instance, God has provided for the gratification of these wants by the creation of precisely the thing the soul demands as its need.* For instance, he has furnished truth to answer the wants of the intellect; beauty to gratify a love for the beautiful; sweet sounds to charm the musical ear; society to answer the cravings of the social instinct; ten thousand sources of amusement to gratify the soul's demands in this respect, and a greater variety of grand and beautiful scenery in different countries to enjoy than it is possible for us to visit, though we spend all our lives in travel.

The reader will see and admit that these demands of the soul, and all others, no matter what their nature, so far as we are able absolutely to know, are answered in every particular, by the production of something in nature, as we before stated, just suited to gratify those demands.

And can it be otherwise with reference to this, the greatest of all needs of the soul,—THE NEED OF ANOTHER EXISTENCE WHEN WE HAVE DONE WITH THIS?

No man knows absolutely that there is any such life. We admit this. But then every man does know that there is no desire of his nature stronger than the desire for another and happier existence. No blessing does he hunger and thirst for as for this. More than this; he feels to know absolutely that this want is *innate in him*—interwoven in the very texture of his spiritual nature, by the Being who gave him his nature. Now can God deny Himself? Can He create a soul that shall be a lie to itself? Has He gratified every other want of body and spirit, and failed to gratify this? The body cries out for food and drink, and these, as we have seen, are supplied in the most wonderful abundance that no physical need may go unsatisfied. The soul hungers and thirsts for a future existence,—for heaven and reunion with dear friends, and love and happiness,—

but there is no future existence to answer this want, —we are told by some,—no heaven, no re-union, no happiness, for death, the very thing the soul most dreads, universally prevails,—all bodies and souls God has made bow before its mandate and are swallowed up forever in the dust and rubbish of the grave!

Other men may believe this, but we cannot; for it gives the lie to the whole order of Providence. The ancient patriarch said in describing the infinite and universal goodness of God, "He openeth His hand and SATISFIETH THE DESIRE OF EVERY LIVING THING." But if there is no future, no life after the death of the body, here is an exception. The greatest and strongest, most vital, inborn and inextinguishable desire of the soul,—a desire that oftentimes manifests itself in tears, and pleadings and anguish, —*is* NOT *satisfied*," but is mocked forever and ever! And this is the *only exception* to the law established by God Himself, and written in characters that are unmistakable all over God's visible creation. Is this reasonable? Can any man, with a feeling, reasoning soul in him, believe it? Our own view is that this universal longing for immortality is God's voice speaking within us and that it will be answered in our dear Father's own good time by the possession of the glorious realities we anticipate in our blessed home in heaven. Never were truer words than these of the poet* so often quoted but with the same

---
* Addison

freshness in proof of the same grand sentiment:—

"Whence this pleasing hope, this fond desire,
This longing after immortality?
Or whence this constant dread, and inward horror,
Of falling into naught?
'*Tis the divinity that stirs within us;*
'Tis HEAVEN ITSELF THAT POINTS OUT OUR HEREAFTER.'

"Oh, I *know* there is a Heaven," exclaimed a dying widow and mother; "I KNOW it, and that my dear husband, and father, and mother, and little Eddy and Mary—my darling children—are *all there.* I FEEL *it in my soul;* and Heaven and the future look very sweet and beautiful to me. Oh, I long to be there. My heart is full of gratitude to the blessed Jesus for the assurance of Heaven and happiness, but at this moment these assurances are but the echo of the certainty of a blessed hereafter which thrill me through and through." And with this hope, amounting to knowledge with her, she fell sweetly asleep in death, to live forever with those so dear to her in the glorious world beyond. If this is *not* so, then God is a lie to Himself. He had given this woman innate yearnings, only to be mocked with the cold fact of absolute death and annihilation! This, in our view, we repeat, is impossible.

CHAPTER III.

"If a man die shall he live again?"

Every creature follows its own Instincts.—Instinct never craves what does not exist.—Illustrations.—The inherent desire of Man is Another Life, and yet Man possesses no indwelling desire for what is not.—The aged Unbeliever.—His Conversion through the presence of ministering angels.—The ecstacy of his joy as he neared the River of Death which he found spanned by the bow of promise.

WE have presented, then, in the preceding chapter, one of the strongest reasons within the scope of our knowledge, independent of the teachings of the Bible, in support of the truth of a future existence. And, following out the leading thought of that chapter to its logical conclusion, we say in addition, that a Being of infinite goodness, guided by infinite wisdom, never would or *could* have created in the nature of his sentient creatures this strong desire for another life *if there is no other life.* He has never implanted in man's nature a *longing for anything that has no existence,* unless indeed, it is true that there is no hereafter. *This is the only exception.* Will our correspondent and all others note this fact, for fact it is. Man possesses no inherent, indwelling longing for anything which has no existence.

The objector may say that men often desire what they do not obtain. And this is true, but they have no inherent desire for anything that is not. Everything that is, craves what its nature demands, and *only* what its nature demands, and it never demands only what has been created to answer that demand. Instinct is inherent—God-given; and every living creature follows its own instincts; but instinct never demands anything that has no existence. Nature never denies itself in this way. The unfledged duckling, as soon as it emerges from its shell, seeks water. It has no knowledge of this element, and yet the water exists. What its nature demands it seeks, and for this only does it seek, and what it instinctively seeks, *it finds*. There are millions of birds of passage, which, as soon as they are fairly grown, quit our cold climate for an atmosphere more congenial. They follow their God-given instincts and what they seek they find; their nature demands *only what exists ; never anything that does not exist.*

Precisely so it is with man. His instincts not only fill him with a dread of death, but with longings for another life. This is what his nature *inherently* craves. Hence, as his nature craves *only what absolutely exists, it follows* AS CERTAINLY AS THE ESTABLISHED LAWS AND METHODS OF GOD ARE UNERRING, THAT THERE IS A HEREAFTER. This is what we believe ; that the birds are not more certain of finding a sunnier home in a more congenial climate by following the unerring instincts of their nature, than is man of finding a more blessed home in that

(3)

world toward which all his thoughts and desires center when he sincerely reflects on the nature of his being and realizes that death is near.

Does the objector say that there are persons who do not, and cannot *believe* in a future life? We grant this, but at the same time we affirm, without fear of a contradiction, that no human being can be found who is sound in mind and body, and who knows enough to comprehend what death and life mean, but dreads the one and desires the other And further, we affirm that no nation or people, however rude, have been found on the face of the earth, where traces of a belief in a future existence of some kind were not discovered. Naiads and Dryads filled the woods and floods of the ancients, and ghosts and spirits have flitted here and there in all the ages of the past, while the fairy and the elf in later days presented a sweeter aspect as descriptions of them flowed from the spirituality of the popular mind. Even on this continent, among the untutored aborigines of the western wilderness, ideas of another existence were prominent. Hence the descriptive words of the poet, so often repeated, but ever fresh because of their beautiful, simple truth :—

> Lo! the poor Indian, whose untutored mind
> Sees God in clouds or hears Him in the wind!
> His soul proud science never taught to stray
> Far as the solar walk or milky way ;
> Yet simple nature to his hope hath given
> Behind the cloud-topt hill some humbler heaven!
> Some safer world in depth of wood embrac'd,
> Some happier island in the watery waste,

> Where slaves once more their native land behold,
> No fiends torment, no Christians thirst for gold!
> *To be* contents his natural desire,
> He asks no angel's wings, no seraph's fire;
> But thinks, admitted to that equal sky,
> His faithful dog shall bear him company.

Here is the thought of the untutored savage relative to another and happier existence when he has done with this; and, we repeat, *all human beings on the face of the earth* are in possession of some such ideas. A happier home in the world to come is awaiting them. They must die, but they shall live again in some more angelic form and sunnier land. If educated under the influence of what are regarded as Christian ideas, they may believe that *others* will suffer in that world to come, but they have no instinctive dread of any great evil befalling *themselves*. At all events, their longings when they die, we repeat, are to live again. This desire is co-eval and co-extensive with the human soul, and hence the great and glorious truth of a future life for every human being is as really and clearly a revelation from God *through the spiritual nature of man, as it is a revelation through the Lord and Savior Jesus Christ*. At all events, this is clear to *our* apprehension. The one revelation confirms and sustains the other. They both teach the same sublime truth. The grand consummation which the soul so devoutly craves, Christ sanctioned and gave the divine promise, not only by his life but by his own resurrection, that all the bright anticipations of the soul with reference to the future shall surely be secured. That *man* really shall not die; that what seems to be death is transition; that the decree,—

> "Dust thou art, to dust returnest,
> Was not spoken of the soul."

So cheer up dear brother or sister whose heart is sad because of bereavement. The precious ones gone are not dead, but are living more really than when they were dwellers in mere forms of flesh. Yes, they are living in a brighter and more blessed world than this; and in God's own good time, you shall go to them, and know them, and they shall know you, and with perfected natures, and improved conditions, you shall experience the exalted joys and enhanced blessings of your higher and diviner life.

O, we repeat, this is what all men *desire*, and the simple fact that there are some who have no faith in the existence of another life is no proof that there is no other life. There are persons who do not believe in the existence of the simplest facts in nature; for instance, in the diurnal revolution of the earth upon its axis; or that the electric current passes thousands of miles through the wire instantaneously, or that millions of living forms exist in a drop of stagnant water, but their skepticism on these matters does not affect the facts asserted. And "shall the unbelief of man make the truth of God [concerning another life] without effect? God forbid. Yea, let God be true but every man a liar!"

If men generally possessed an inborn dread of living again, or innate spirit of opposition to such a condition, *this* would be proof against the doctrine of immortality. But, as we have seen, their most ardent aspirations are all the other way; so that often the very men who say they do not, and cannot *believe* in a future existence, experience the most fearful dread of death, and the most earnest *desire* to live, either here or hereafter. We have seen such men. We cannot say we have met with persons of the other sex who had no faith in another life; but we have been personally intimate with several men, —some of them men of reading and culture,—who openly denied the truth of a future existence. With them the Bible was a sham and Christ a myth; and yet, they all, without an exception, desired more than all things the truth of the very thing their judgments rejected. There was one, especially, to whom our mind now reverts, eighty years of age, who had no faith in another existence. Death, in his apprehension, was a thing absolute and positive. When his heart should cease to beat, he said, then *he* should be dead, soul and body, and never again would he know anything or sense anything or have affection for anything, any more than a dead horse or ox, or so much inanimate clay. "Death," he would often say, "will snuff me out like snuffing out a candle, and that will be the end of me!" And yet, no man apparently ever felt a greater dread of death or a more ardent desire to live *somewhere*. For years, he was exceedingly careful of his health. If he accidentally wet his feet or otherwise exposed himself to taking cold, or at any time felt an unusual pain or ache, he would hasten to his home in alarm, and use every precaution against sickness, lest sickness should lead to death, and death was annihilation. He often said he should be willing to be chained to a post in the open air, enduring the heat of summer and the peltings of the storms of winter, and subsist on a cracker a day with a little cold water, from year to year and from age to age, if he could only be permitted to live, the thought of death and annihilation was so dreadful to him!

It will be seen that this man in his thought denied the "divinity within him." His soul yearned for a hereafter. It cried out in a voice of agony against death and for life immortal, which demonstrates that only immortality will satisfy the demands of such a soul. And the reality of this great truth, strange as it may seem, was shown him before he was called to pass through the shadows of the dark valley, for when he drew near the river's brink, its darkness was dispelled. All mist was gone, and the river which all along had appeared to his misguided apprehension so troubled and formidable, was narrow and placid, and spanned by the bright bow of promise. Heaven seemed to open to his spiritual vision. He gazed intently into the beautiful vista before him, and said he saw Jesus and a shining throng of glorified spirits, and among them his angel wife who had long since gone before him, and his first born child,—a dear daughter,—and his darling grandchild, and a host of dear friends! "Oh, how beautiful! how blessed!" he exclaimed, and the angels took him by the hand to help him over. He seemed to feel their kiss, and was so astonished that others could not see what he saw! His soul was in raptures because it already possessed what it had longed for, and suffered and agonized for.

And so he died,—or, rather, so he was resurrected into another and more glorious existence, and by laws as natural, as real and as unerring, we believe, as those which control our birth into the present existence.

But of this we will speak in another chapter. In the meantime, will our correspondent consider carefully that his skepticism concerning another life weighs nothing against his ardent longings for another existence. All he possesses on earth he is willing to surrender, he says, to feel and know that he and his shall live again. God grant this boon may yet be his to enjoy.

CHAPTER IV.

What is the Resurrection? How and when shall it Transpire?

The common Views.—Unbelief of Paul.—His strong Faith after His Conversion.—Distinction between the Man and the House he Lives in.—Luminous Views of Paul.—Great and Beautiful Truth perfectly answering the spiritual needs of the soul.

WE have now seen that such are the indwelling longings of the soul and the corresponding provisions of Providence to answer all created needs, that there must be somewhere another existence for man when he has done with the present; and if so, the question arises, *what is the process by or through which he enters upon that existence?* This is a question which not only interests but puzzles many minds. Such has been the character of their religious education, that to them the whole subject of the resurrection is an incomprehensible mystery. If their is a heaven *how* and *when* do we reach it? Clergymen, whose office it is to console the bereaved, standing over the earthly remains of dear ones departed, define the resurrection to be a resuscitation of our veritable bodies at the end of all things, and more than intimate that not until this great event transpires through the opening of literal graves, can any enter that home of many mansions prepared in heaven for God's great family; and yet, perhaps, before they have closed their remarks, they will speak of the cherished departed as having already entered the world of bliss and met others gone before, in the sweet company of whom they are now participating in the enjoyment of the glad beauties and fresh delights of heaven.

Here is contradiction,—and contradiction involving mystery, they say. The resurrection and the happiness of heaven involve the resuscitation of the body, and yet here lies the body of the dear one before them, still and cold, clad in the sable habiliments of death. How then can the above theory be true? And by what possibility can man live in one place while his dead body is in another? Such impossibilities, mysteries and contradictions, notwithstanding their longings for the life to come, they cannot and will not believe.

But we do not think reasonable men will thus object to the true doctrine of the resurrection and what it anticipates and involves. There have always been unbelievers with regard to the subject. Paul, himself, the great apostle to the Gentiles, for a while, was a notorious opposer of the doctrine of another existence; but after his conversion by the sudden appearance of the spirit of Christ, which shone round about him like a flood of light, and spoke to him in an audible voice, though "he could see no man," so clear were his conceptions and so strong his faith in heaven and glory, that to him it amounted to certainty; and hence became the great thought of his life. Everywhere he went he preached the Gospel, and the doctrine of the resurrection as the foundation of that gospel. Never did he omit this; because to omit this would be omitting Christ who was the "Resurrection and the Life:" It would be omitting God and heaven and glory.

But Paul had no idea of going into the grave on the death of his body and there amidst its decay and corruption, waiting to the end of time for the consummation of this great event but said, "We do know that if our earthly house of this tabernacle were dissolved [in the grave] *we* have a building of God, an house not made with hands, eternal in the heavens. * * Therefore we are always confident, *knowing* that, whilst we are at home in the body, we are absent from the Lord. * * We are confident, I say, and willing rather to be *absent from the body* AND BE PRESENT WITH THE LORD." * Paul could live, then, independently of his natural body;—live with Christ. This was what he believed; yea, it was what he KNEW. Hence, what we call death had no terrors for him. When his enemies combined to kill him, he saw not death or the grave, but only Christ and heaven and glory, and was filled with divine power. He was victor over death, through faith that amounted to knowledge. And yet the world all around him was filled

---
* 2 Cor. 5; 1:6-7.

with skepticism, as it is this day, concerning this great subject, because it comprehended it not.

But, as we have seen, men are not skeptical with reference to this subject, from choice. Nothing more seriously disturbs the tranquillity of the soul than the thought of death and annihilation, and gladly would they believe in a future life if it could appear reasonable to them and they could see sufficient evidence of its reality. But this has never been offered them. It is true, Christianity teaches it, but they have no proof of the truths of Christianity. To them, the New Testament is no authority. Christ may have lived subsequently to his death on the cross; or he may not have lived. Eighteen hundred years have passed since his crucifixion and it is now very difficult to determine how much we should believe or reject of the history which purports to tell of him;—his life, his doctrine, his death, resurrection and ascension. They say, if the mysteries referred to could be explained and they could discover anything in nature,—in the developments of science,—in the powers of the soul,— or in reason,—to confirm the idea of another life and that heaven is our home, they would receive it with the greatest avidity and delight.

We propose then, in what we now offer, to confine our reflections entirely to this phase of the subject. In previous chapters we have shown what the soul *demands.* We will now first briefly state what we conceive to be the Christian doctrine of the resurrection, by which it will be seen *how* and *when* men enter on another existence, and then inquire if there is not something in the nature of things as they exist around us, in reason, in science and in the nature of the soul, which will, at least, serve to strengthen our faith in this comforting doctrine, which will be seen to answer precisely the demands of the soul. And we propose to do this as much for the gratification of the Christian as for the enlightenment of the skeptic, for the reason that such is the nature of this sublime question, involving interests so vital, that the very instincts of the soul delight to seek for confirmations of its truth from every source no matter what its nature.

What, then, is the Christian doctrine of the Resurrection?

We answer, first, negatively, that it is *not* the opening of literal graves and the resuscitation of literal bodies,—some thousands or millions of ages hence,—clothing these bones again with flesh and blood and sinews, and re-animating them with physical life, as this would be utterly inconsistent with every development in nature;—but it *is* the rising of our spiritual being into a new form and condition of existence, when it has done with the body, just as the butterfly emerges from the gross material of the worm, and, clothed in a new and beautiful body, flits from flower to flower, or soars aloft in the sunlight of heaven. Through a process entirely natural, but wonderful and inconceivable by man, it has been resurrected, transformed, "gone up higher" and will never again descend to its former condition of a worm, or enter the body from which it has been liberated. Its existence is one of greater purity, beauty and delight. By the change it has experienced, it is fitted for the new and more advanced sphere it occupies, and has no more need of the body it has left, than the bird of paradise has of the shell from which it emerges in the process of incubation.

Neither shall we have need of the tabernacles of flesh and blood we now inhabit, when, through the death of the body and the wonderful process of the resurrection, we have passed from mortality into immortality, and from the earthly into the heavenly. We say WE; and we mean by this to confine our identity as persons *to our spirits*. The body is not *the man*. It is simply the house he lives in while connected with material things. It belongs to him; he does not belong to it, and desertion from it is no proof of death or annihilation. We once called at the old home of some very dear friends. We found its doors and shutters closed, the building dilapidated, and the stillness of death reigning on all around. Are our kind old friends all *dead*? was our inward ejaculation. Not at all. They had simply deserted the old, tumble-down tenement for a paradise of a home on the brow of the hill beyond, where we found them, surrounded with elegance and beauty, and in the rich enjoyment of health and the delights of peace.

No, we repeat, the body is not *the man*. You may sever his hands, arms, feet and indeed all his limbs, and yet you have not touched *him*. These bodily organs belong to him; he does not belong to them. They move at his volition; he never at theirs, for they have none. There is no thought, no affection, no power to will, or ability to reason, in a man's hand, or foot, or skull, or in the fleshy substance of the brain. The man lives, indeed, while a man, and *only* a man, in connection with these bodily organs, and yet in a sense personally distinct from them. He says, "this is *my* hand," "*my* foot," "*my* eye," "*my* ear," as if he were distinct from them. These organs though belonging to him, sense nothing;—*he* everything. The ear does not hear, the eye see, the nose smell, or the brain reason. *The soul*, which is supposed to be incorporated in some mysterious manner with the brain, reasons. It is the soul which sees and hears and smells through the instrumentality of these bodily organs, and when they have served man the purpose of God's design in their creation, and death has released him from them, he will never more have use for them. They will return to dust, their native element, to be incorporated into new organisms, while *he* will pass into a more perfect condition of spiritual existence, and clothed upon with a new body, divine, spiritual, celestial, he will be fitted for the new, advanced and exalted sphere into which he shall be raised, when the **unveiled splendors of God's vast universe shall dawn** upon the soul, and it shall be free to go upward and onward, from strength to strength, from beauty to beauty, from glory to glory without hindrance and without limit.

And *this* is the resurrection as revealed by both Christ and Paul. The promise of Jesus to the thief upon the cross, was, "To-day shalt thou be with me in Paradise." * By "Paradise" Christ certainly meant the *home and state of the blest*, though in what the *locality* of that state consists, no one knows. There can be no doubt in the mind of the Christian, but this promise of our dear Lord was verified, so that on the very day of the crucifixion, both Christ and the malefactor entered a condition of exquisite delight, in the realms of divine spirituality. And yet, it is equally certain that their *bodies*, held in the cold embrace of death, remained hanging upon the cross all that day, which shows, not only the distinction which Christ made between himself and his body, but the wonderful transformation achieved though unseen, by the power and process of the resurrection. Their *bodies* were lifeless and yet *they* lived more really than ever before in Paradise.

So of Paul, whose joyful anticipation was to live in the spirit world with Christ when his enemies should destroy the tabernacle he then inhabited; and who frequently declared that death would unclothe him; that is, remove his old, mortal garment, while the resurrection would clothe him with an immortal

---
* Luke's Gospel. 23:43.

vestment, pure and beautiful. His luminous declarations on the subject, as contained in his letter to the Corinthian church, are full of cheering truth. Some men will say, "*How* are the dead [those who are dying] raised up, and with what body do they come?" He answers, "Thou fool, that which thou sowest is not quickened except it die; and that which thou sowest, thou sowest *not that body that shall be*, * * but God giveth it a body as it hath pleased Him, and to every seed His own body. * * So also is the resurrection of the dead [or those who die]. It is sown in corruption, it is raised in incorruption; it is sown in dishonor, it is raised in glory; [The reader will please notice that the verbs employed are all in the present tense, showing that the raising is progressive as is the sowing.] It is sown in weakness, it is raised in power; it is sown a natural body, it is raised a spiritual body. There is a natural body and there is a spiritual body. * * As is the earthy such are they also that are earthy, and as is the heavenly such are they also that are heavenly; and as we have borne the image of the earthy we shall also bear the image of the heavenly."

Here is Paul's sublime and beautiful idea of the resurrection. He then possessed a mortal body. This was an earthly "image." When death should come, and disrobe him, followed by the enrobing process of the resurrection, the change would take place which he describes, and he would possess an immortal vestment, allied to the heavenly. He would be glorious, spiritual, powerful and blessed. No longer bound by the gross elements of the earthy, he would be capable of ranging through the immensity of the universe at will; advanced in knowledge he would have the ability to comprehend the more complex laws of nature and of enjoying the sublime privilege of communing with angels and of cultivating the diviner elements of his nature forever.

How grand this truth. How sweet and blessed the consummation it anticipates. The reader will see *when* and *how* God's children enter the future life—the heavenly home. Oh, that these ideas could universally prevail. How speedily would they disrobe death of its terrors, surround the grave with a halo of glory, and pointing to the bright world above, say to the bereaved and dying, "Your dear ones live. Ye shall go to them but they shall not return to you."

CHAPTER V.

The Resurrection in Harmony with Nature.

Paul's reasoning with Agrippa who denied the doctrine of the Resurrection.—What is there in this doctrine more difficult to comprehend or harder to believe than many other things in Nature.—The Resurrection not against Nature, but in harmony with it.—Wonderful transformation of the Worm into the Butterfly.—The Resurrection a Birth of the Soul into Another Life.—Shall we retain consciousness during the process of the Resurrection.

WE have now seen what the resurrection is, and would ask the candid reader what there is in it which is difficult to comprehend, or hard to believe. We are informed that, on a certain occasion, Paul was taken by his enemies, because of his bold and positive defence of the truth of Christ's resurrection and the sublime doctrine of the ultimate home in heaven, of all God's great family, and brought into the presence of Agrippa, where, in a masterly speech, he again lifted up his voice in support of these divine sentiments, during which he turned to Agrippa, and knowing his skepticism on the subject, asked, "Why should it be thought a thing incredible with *you* that God should raise the dead ?" How significant this question under the circumstances! All Judea was then ringing with the great event of Christ's resurrection. Its truth was so palpable that even Agrippa dare not deny it.

He had faith in the true God whose *wisdom, power* and *goodness* he believed to be *infinite*. How could *such* a Being create a human soul and fill it with perpetual longings for a future life, and yet fail so to ordain the laws of its spiritual being as to secure precisely this result? To say that he could, would be "incredible;" but to say that he had placed in the soul the seeds of immortality that by the hidden forces of their own nature, would develop into higher and diviner beings on the death and dissolution of this mortal body, is just what the apostle knew to be entirely in harmony with the goodness of God, the nature of man, and to be true in point of fact. And yet, with Agrippa this fact was "incredible." That is, it was too extraordinary and improbable to admit of belief.

Some who peruse these pages may entertain similar views and feelings. If so, permit us to ask again, what there is in it *more* "incredible" than in a thousand things constantly transpiring around us in the visible world, the truth of which we never doubt? Do you say it is *unnatural* and therefore incredible? On the contrary, nothing is more natural. The common notion of the resuscitation of our physical bodies some millions of ages hence is unnatural, we grant, and contrary to every development in the visible creation; but not so the system revealed by the apostle. Being born into a higher condition of spiritual existence, is as really the result of the action of certain fixed laws, or inherent forces in our being, as is our birth into this world, or as is the process by which the worm is transformed into the butterfly. We have before spoken of this fact in natural history, and refer to it again, rather than to any other similar development in nature, because it so perfectly illustrates the truth we wish to impress. No man or woman of intelligence will deny *the fact* of the transformation of the worm to which we refer, or that it is accomplished through the inherent forces of its own nature operating to this end; and yet, the change produced is just as wonderful, and the process by which it is accomplished is just as incredible as that which takes place with the soul in its resurrection out of this physical organism, into one of spirituality and glory. We have watched the change to which we refer, on several occasions, with the greatest wonder and delight, an instance of which we will describe.

A few years ago, we chanced to notice two large, dark-colored, nearly black, and very unsightly worms or caterpillars crawling upon the ground near the roots of an apple tree in our garden. They were too offensive to the sight to touch with the fingers. Making use of a leaf and a stick we secured them. Putting them into a large tumbler with a few pieces of the leaves of the tree under which they were found, for food, we covered the glass and placed it on the writing table in our library. The worms soon devoured the leaves and we gave them a fresh supply. In a few days, in a manner wonderfully curious, each wove for itself a shroud. It was a kind of net work of gossamer, silken in appearance, with which each enrobed itself so entirely as to be utterly hidden from sight. They were now motionless, yea, as "still as death." To every outward appearance, *they were* DEAD. This drapery was their tomb, but it was also the cradle of the new life to be developed from the old organism. We now uncovered the glass. How long a time it required to perfect the work of transformation we have forgotten; but we shall never forget the delight and astonishment with which we were thrilled on a bright and charming morning, when we suddenly opened the door of the library and discovered a most gorgeous and beautiful butterfly of the largest species, whirling about the room in graceful curves, seeming to be in the perfect enjoyment of its new and advanced existence. It soon alighted on a flower at the window. We approached the tumbler and were again delighted to notice that the resurrection process of the other was completed, and the butterfly, equally large and brilliant with the first, sat upon the edge of the tumbler balancing its wings as if about to test its ability to use them. It soon went in quest of its mate. On examining the inside of the glass, we discovered the grosser remains of the two worms which had thus been metamorphosed into two brilliant cherubim. How wonderful and incomprehensible the process! What a change in the outward appearance of the two insects! How loathsome the worm; but how charmingly attractive the butterfly! What golden colors; how brilliant and gorgeous! Before, they were offensive caterpillars, crawling in the dust. Now we opened the window and they soared aloft in the beauty and glory of the sunlight.

And all this wonderful development from the nature of a worm! The reader does not dispute the fact we record. It is not too astonishing for his credulity. Why not believe a similar truth of himself and those he loves, when God has assured us that we have the elements of immortality within us, and that on the death of our bodies, through the inherent forces of our nature, we shall surely develop into diviner beings and have existence in that house not made with hands eternal in the heavens? The one is no more inexplicable or impossible than the other. The process of the resurrection of man is as natural as that of the transformation of the worm. We are all born into the present life through the operation of certain inherent forces. These laws are universally the same in all persons in the process of production and reproduction. They show no respect of persons. So with the birth which ushers the soul into a purely spiritual existence. The laws which govern it are precisely the same in their operations with all. The resurrection is, therefore, no miracle, but the result of certain established laws which are natural, over which we have no control.

If physical life is positively removed from a human body, and again restored, *that* is a miracle, or a deviation from what are the established laws of nature. The established laws of nature say that when physical life is extinct in a human body, decomposition shall follow, and no natural power of which man has any knowledge, can restore its vitality and consciousness. What he regards as *supernatural* energy is necessary to produce such an effect. Christ re-animated the dead body of Lazarus and that of the son of the widow of Nain, with physical vitality and mental consciousness. His own natural body was also raised from the tomb. These were miracles, necessary at the time, as Christ explained to those who witnessed the wonderful works he did, "to the end, that they might believe." But the resurrection of those who are daily passing into a higher form of spiritual existence is no more a miracle than is the birth of those who are just entering this state of existence.

Indeed, the resurrection is a birth of the spiritual of man's nature into another life, as really as the transformation of the worm is the birth of the butterfly into its new and advanced sphere. In the latter case our senses take cognizance of the wonderful change produced, and, hence, we do not doubt the truth of what we witness. Could our mortal vision as plainly discern the spiritual, our firm belief is, that those who stand weeping around the death-bed of those dear to them,—witnessing the life of the body gradually ebbing away, till the heart ceases entirely to pulsate, when the breath stops and the eyes close in death, they would see the process of the resurrection as it progressed and would be thrilled, through and through, with astonishment and delight at what they beheld. They would witness the soul with its spiritual body,—for "there *is* a spiritual body, and there *is* a natural body,"*—rising calmly and sweetly in brightness and glory, from out of the physical body, in fashion of the human form and yet in likeness of Christ's glorious body, all sparkling with celestial life. In some cases it may occupy hours for the completion of this birth,—which is the perfection of the new birth,—but when this transpires and the life-cord which unites the earthly with the heavenly, is severed, then the work of the resurrection is perfected, —the soul is fully liberated from the clogs of earth, and can go and come, appear and disappear, with the effort of the will, "as quick as thought," and without regard to space or material hindrance.

We repeat, if the mourning soul could really discern all this with his natural sense;—could behold the bright spirits of dear departed friends from their celestial home, hovering over the death-bed of those about to leave them, waiting to welcome them to their new world of delights, how would their mourning be turned to joy, and all their ideas of death, now so dreadful and appalling, be changed to those of wonder and delight.

What we have written above on this subject, is

---

* 1 Cor. 15:44.

not what we *know*, but what we *believe*, based on deductions from the sacred Word. This belief has afforded us great peace in seasons of deepest sorrow. We present them as a solace to other troubled souls. And pursuing the subject in this direction a little further, would say that we have been asked if, in our view, the soul becomes *unconscious* at the time of death, and during the process of the resurrection as described in the foregoing. We can simply give our belief on this subject, as on the other, which is, that some are in a condition of unconsciousness in passing from the earthly into the heavenly, while others are vividly awake. The apostle says, in describing the resurrection process, "We shall not *all sleep*, but we shall *all be changed*,*

---

* The common interpretation of these words is that "We shall not all *die*,"—the word *sleep*, as used by the apostle, being supposed to signify *death*. This exposition, though sustained by Biblical critics of all denominations, so far as we have the means of knowing, was never satisfactory to us, for the reason, first, that all people then existing on the earth did die; and second, the apostle had just declared in this chapter the truth of the death of ALL *men*. Hence, when he said, "Behold I shew you a mystery; we shall not all *sleep*, but we shall all be *changed*," he could not have meant they shall not all *die*, and that *this* was the "mystery" to which he referred: but he did mean, as we apprehend, that in dying, and during the process of the resurrection which should follow, they should not, as we say above, "all sleep" the sleep of unconsciousness. This view is not only reasonable but it harmonizes all the instruction of the context. And at the risk of being charged with favoring spiritualism, we are inclined to relate the incident by which we were put in posession of the leading thought embraced in the foregoing. It has always been a rule of our life to investigate all questions and phenomena that professed to afford testimony favoring the truth of a hereafter.

Some years ago, we chanced to hear a lecture from the distinguished Judge Edmonds of New York city, on what he called "The Facts of Spiritualism." He was a gentleman of character and of unquestioned veracity. Among other things related by him as facts, he stated that in a moment, in the twinkling of an eye, at the last trump."* The meaning of which is, that when death comes to each one of us,—an event which is God's last summons,—or "trump" [the word is used metaphorically] to us,—"we shall not all sleep,"—that is, go into a condition of unconsciousness, resembling "sleep;" but we SHALL ALL BE CHANGED,—just as he had already described,—from mortality into immortality, from the dishonorable to the glorious, etc., "in a moment, in the twinkling of an eye." Not

---

just previously, Mr. I. T. Hopper, the excellent old Quaker of New York, for a long time keeper of a Pennsylvania Penitentiary, and so celebrated as the prisoners' friend in New York city, was sick unto death. His residence was not far from that of Mrs. Lydia Maria Child. the distinguished authoress, one of his warmest and dearest friends. In her parlor a select company of Spiritualists, he said, often had sittings. One evening, when Mr. Hopper was expected to survive but a brief time, he (Judge Edmonds) was present at Mrs. Child's, and as soon as a circle was formed, what purported to be the spirit of Mr Hopper communicated to them the fact of what he called his "great change;" and said that it occurred three hours previously, at which time he was released from his body. "But," said he, "not for a moment was I unconscious. All the family surrounded my bed and with tears and faces of sadness were looking at my body and lamenting what they call *my death*. They tell everybody who comes to the door to inquire, that I am dead, when the truth is, I never before knew as I now know *what life means*. Please go and tell them not to feel so badly about it. It is a'l right, and further I wish to say that I now know what the apostle meant when he said, 'We shall not *all* SLEEP, but we shall *all be* CHANGED.' I have experienced the wondrous *change*, though I was not for a moment asleep."

Judge Edmonds said that they hastened to the home of the good, old man and found, indeed, that he had forsaken his wasted form as described.

We cannot vouch for the truth of this story, though we have no disposition to ridicule or deny it. Such relations from such a source strengthen our faith in another life. But what we wish specially to say, is, that on investigation we have found no more consistent interpretation of the words of the apostle referred to, than was thus singularly brought to our mind.

* 1 Cor. 15:51-52.

that the entire work of the resurrection, or the birth of the soul into the life to come, shall literally take place "in the twinkling of an eye," but the completion of the work, which is the severing of the lifecord that connects the earthly with the heavenly nature, shall be instantaneous; *then* the great change described shall be perfected. The apostle continues, "FOR this corruptible *must* put on incorruption, and this mortality must put on immortality. So when this corruptible shall have put on incorruption, and this mortal shall have put on immortality, THEN shall be brought to pass the saying that is written, 'DEATH IS SWALLOWED UP IN VICTORY.'"*

How grand and blessed the consummation reached through *death*,—the very thing we dread,—and the power of the resurrection. With every soul *this corruptible* MUST put on incorruption, and *this mortal* MUST *put on immortality*. This is indispensable, but in the change, the sleep of unconsciousness in every case is not indispensable. Some shall be unconscious and others as vividly awake as at any other moment. We have witnessed enough at the bedside of the dying greatly to strengthen us in a belief of the truth of what Paul here affirms. Some die in a condition of stupor; others remain in a condition of unconsciousness for days, till within a short time of death, when they will suddenly arouse, perhaps sit up in bed, converse of the delightful things they have seen and heard; take leave of all the family

---
* 1 Cor. 15:53-55.

in tones of the greatest cheerfulness, and draw their last breath perhaps in the very midst of a sentence; while others will remain entirely conscious during all their sickness, their minds growing more and more vividly awake, as their end approaches, and so they die with eyes bright and thoughts lucid. In such cases, it seems to us, consciousness must remain as the soul rises into another and diviner life. We now recall a scene we witnessed in Taunton, Mass., during our pastorate there years ago, which made a deep impression on our mind at the time. We stood at the bedside of a young man,*—twenty-seven years of age,—whose bodily frame was greatly emaciated with consumption, and yet his mind was vividly alive to all around. His father had already gone to his home in heaven, and the aged mother followed soon after. His only brother was present, and stood directly by his side. We were near the foot of his bed. He was looking at us with a calm, patient look, and talking about dying and going to his home above. Neither of us thought his change so near. He soon looked steadily into his brother's face, and taking him suddenly by the hand, said, "Charles, I am going. Good-by." And nodding to us,—"Good-by, Brother Quinby,"—he breathed perhaps twice and was dead. We do not mean this. His *body* was dead. We could not feel that *he* was dead. It seemed to us that he was res-

---

* Wm. Foster. The brother to whom we refer as being present, was Charles Foster, Esq., now, and for a long time, a leading member of the Universalist church in Taunton.

urrected into a higher life, and without so much as a moment's unconsciousness.* He was now "absent from the body." The lustre of the eye was gone. The ear heard no sound. The heart had ceased to beat; and yet we believe he saw with greater clearness than ever before, and heard what he never before heard,—the enchanting melody of celestial music. If Christ and the malefactor entered Paradise, and into the enjoyment of heavenly rest and peace on the day of their death, why not this young man, and all our dear ones, who pass from our embrace. This is what the hope of Christ, as revealed in the New Testament, unfolds. Do not weep then, my brother or sister, because death has visited your home and taken those very dear to you, for they "are risen," and now live in company with the lost and loved and beautiful, where there is re-union of all the sundered ties of affection, and where "God shall wipe away all tears from their eyes; and there shall be no more death, neither sorrow, nor crying, neither shall there be any more pain, for the former things are passed away."† Yes

"We know when the silver cord is loosed,
When the vail is rent away,
Not long and dark will the passage be
To the realms of endless day.

---

* When the distinguished Rev. JOHN TODD, D. D., for thirty years pastor of the Congregationalist church in Pittsfield, Mass., died a few years ago, the last words he uttered were "Glory! glory! glory!" in the midst of which he ceased to breathe. He believed that on the death of his body, his eyes would open on scenes of celestial beauty and glory, and we have no doubt but his expectation was fully realized precisely as he anticipated.

† Revelations 21:4.

> "The eye that shuts in the dying hour,
> Will open the next in bliss;
> The welcome will sound in the heavenly world,
> Ere the farewell is hushed in this."

Numerous are the instances recorded where the dying not only felt a certainty of being raised immediately to Heaven and glory, but where Heaven and glory were opened to them and were brought so near them that they seemed to gaze upon the enrapturing sight, and hear enchanting, celestial sounds. Dear ones who had passed to the higher life, in angelic purity now beckoned them, and were eager to welcome them to the abodes of unalloyed bliss. We once witnessed a scene* of this character and never shall we forget the impression which it made on our heart. God's name be praised, there is a future— a blessed, glorious future—for all His children! Then

> "Let us not mourn; though life may bring us sorrow;
> Soon shal we cast aside the cumbrous clay;
> We have a hope—a glorious hope to-morrow—
> A Home in Heaven—a Home of constant day.
>
> "A Home where death can never enter;
> It stands untouched by the flight of years,
> A stream of bliss is glittering in its center;
> 'Tis God's own city, unalloyed by tears."

---

* See pages 100-103 of this book.

CHAPTER VI.

Doctrine of the Resurrection Strengthened by a Further Appeal to Nature.

Men will believe in the Truths of Nature and yet deny the truth of their own nature.—Facts in the Natural World.—Laws which govern the Spiritual do certainly exist.—Change in the Body.—Change in the Soul.—Wonders in the Visible World.—Why not Wonders in the Spiritual World?

THE views thus far presented may appear reasonable to the reader, and yet he may doubt the reality of the leading fact stated,—to wit: that the spiritual of man's nature possesses inherent forces, which, operating as we have described, result in the resurrection of the soul into a higher and diviner condition. Will he permit us, therefore, to lead him a step farther out into the arena of nature as it exists around us, for the purpose of gathering corresponding facts in support of the sublime truth we present? We would not make these pages heavy with attempts at profound reasoning or subtile logic, but it is our earnest desire to convince those of weak faith in God, and who possess little or no hope of a hereafter, of that grand gospel truth, which is "as an anchor of the soul, sure and steadfast," and we would employ all reasonable means to effect this happy result. The reader believes *in the truths of nature*, but he has no faith that man possesses in *his* nature the God-given forces that, operating silently and invisibly, result in the development of the soul into celestial conditions. We have seen the teachings of nature on this subject, as manifested in the inherent forces in the being of the worm, that transformed it into a living existence as much more beautiful than the loathsome worm from which it was developed, as an angel is more beautiful than man. But let us look a little further and we shall find that nature and science never disprove Christianity, but contain much to substantiate it. For everywhere around us we shall find the existence of the same invisible law in operation, of which we speak.

Science has revealed the fact that "in the natural world there are two entirely distinct classes of existences. First, certain *material forms;* and, second, certain *forces*, which lie underneath and are immediately active in producing and sustaining those forms." Now while the operation of these *forces* are invisible to the eye, their *effects* are everywhere discernible. For illustration, we take an acorn. This has material form; but who that has no knowledge of the fact, would believe the oak lies folded up in that little shell? We place the nut in the ground, and what are the effects which follow? After lapse of time the acorn germinates,—a sprout is produced; then come the branches, leaves, blossoms, fruit, each in turn, till at length there stands before us a broad, majestic tree with its huge limbs and cooling shade.

Here are the effects which have certainly transpired. What produced them? The hidden forces contained in the elements of nature, for these forces are but laws in activity. But notice: while there is one force operating to produce a new organism, there is another force operating to destroy the old organism. If, after placing the acorn in the ground, we take occasion to watch the progress of germination and growth, we shall find the grosser material of the nut turning to decay as the living germ develops its vitality and indwelling forces, and in a comparatively brief space of time, dissolving into dust.

And here we discover the basis of the apostle's allegorical reasoning of the germinating process of grain sown in the earth, in answer to the question, "what *body*" we shall bear in the life to come. "Thou fool,"* he says, "that which thou sowest is not *quickened* [into new life and growth and beauty] *except it die.*" Ah! yes, dear reader, will you bear this great truth in mind as death appears before you as an appalling monster? You fear him, and yet you should ever remember that the "body"—the *outside*, or lobes of the kernel *must die*, that the inward germ may develop into diviner life and being. There is no other possible process by which we can reach the spirituality and glory of heaven.

---

* 1 Cor. 15:36.

Said our dear Lord, "Verily, verily, I say unto you, except a corn of wheat fall into the ground and *die, it abideth alone ;* but IF IT DIE *it bringeth forth much fruit.*" The apostle makes an application of this simile to man in the resurrection-state, and says "So also is the resurrection of the dead [or those who die] ; it is sown in corruption, it is raised in incorruption ; it is sown in dishonor, it is raised in glory ; it is sown in weakness, it is raised in power; it is sown a natural body, it is raised a spiritual body ;" and by this application he demonstrates the important and interesting philosophical truth to which we just now referred, viz.: that the *spiritual* of man's nature is just as certainly under the control of certain fixed forces which lie hidden in its being as is the *physical.* We repeat, we would not attempt to define the nature of the soul or explain *what it is.* Every man knows it is *something.* The things which are seen are *temporal,*—the things unseen are *eternal.* We know not the nature of its essence. but we believe the human soul to be a positive organism,—more really so than the body,— and no matter how subtile or ethereal, it must be under the control, and subject to the influence of laws as certainly as all else God has created. We have spoken of the changes which are constantly going on in the material world, and which are produced by the unseen forces combined with itself. These forces operate in countless forms. Throw a stone into the air,—what we call gravitation brings it back to the earth. The needle points to the pole. Heat generates steam when applied to water. Cold converts water into ice. Flowers, plants and trees spring from the earth in endless variety,—again they decay and crumble to dust. Here are *effects* which every man beholds, but the *causes* are utterly hidden from his natural vision. But if intelligent he will not doubt the certainty of their existence. Indeed he *knows* they exist, notwithstanding they are invisible, and notwithstanding no human wisdom has ever been sufficient to divine their nature or the mode of their operation.

So with the forces innate in our spiritual being. "The dust shall return to the earth as it was, *and the spirit to the God who gave it.*" When what we call death takes place with a man, a change is produced in his body. We know this for it is perceptible to all, and there is nothing difficult to believe about it, because it is an occurrence so common. But the dissolution of the body does not necessarily involve the destruction of the soul, any more than the dissolution of the grosser material of the acorn involves the dissolution of the germ which develops into a tree. The soul possesses elements of its own, divine, indestructible, immortal, and when it is "unclothed" by the death of the body, it is resolved into the "heavenly," and clothed upon with its ethereal vestments, through the instrumentality of the forces which are incorporated in its being. As we have before shown, it unfolds like a beautiful flower in the glowing, strengthening sunshine, opening its petals, reaching out its expanding energies, all the time gathering to itself from the ethereal element around, and the spiritual forces within, its pure, immortal garment, till the work of the resurrection is complete, when it is fitted to its new, celestial and more glorious sphere. It now has no more affinity for its former rude body on earth, or desire to re-enter it, than the gorgeous butterfly we have described, did it possess a reasoning mind, would have to return to its former habitation of the loathsome worm crawling in dust and filth.

Does any one say that he can have no faith in what we have now affirmed because he can discover nothing of it with his natural vision while the process of the resurrection is going forward?—that his friends have died in his presence;—he has stood weeping over them and witnessed their last look, their last respiration and seen their unconscious bodies dressed in the habiliments of death, but he never could discover the existence of anything spiritual about them after their hearts had ceased to pulsate with physical life? But did he *before?* Did he ever see a spirit? You may say that you do not believe in the existence of spirits. But you do. You know that your hand or foot or skull does not think or reason or love; that this ability belongs alone to the soul, and hence you feel that you are in possession of a soul. All your friends and acquaintances are in possession of souls, and you *know it*, and yet you never saw a soul. Will you deny the existence of *everything* you cannot *see*? You are every moment breathing an element that gives vitality and vigor to your physical system. You know it exists but you cannot see it. Electricity pervades every part of the visible universe. When under the direction and control of man, it is made to pass from point to point, through the electric wires, thousands of miles, instantaneously. Will you deny the existence of this element because you cannot discern it with your natural vision? If so, then, for the same reason, you would deny the process by which the worm is transformed into a butterfly, and you yourself were brought into being. Yea, you would deny the existence of all the unseen forces in operation in the production of vegetation, and in the revolution of the heavenly bodies.

We cannot see the spirit during the resurrection process, as this boon is not granted us under ordinary conditions, but this is *no reason for rejecting the fact of the resurrection.*

Nor should we reject anything in the development of nature or science and call it false or impossible because we cannot *comprehend* it. The man who acts upon this principle, must make the rule universal, and so reject *all* which does not come within the sphere of his capacity. And then what would be left? For, after all, how little of nature do we really understand?

A little flower of many hues,—very delicate and

very beautiful,—almost ethereal, and of sweetest fragrance,—unfolds in your conservatory. *Whence* came it, and *how?* You place it in your parlor and for days the fragrance which it exhales will perfume the room, filling it day and night, with sweetest odor, and yet, on a careful microscopic examination, not the least possible diminution of it is discernible. Who is able to comprehend this wonderful fact in nature? Another flower and another still are produced, side by side with the first, till hundreds are developed from the same elements of earth, air, and water, and yet no two are similar in color, foliage, texture or fragrance. How wonderful! We ask again who can comprehend how and whence they came? No man. Even Solomon, in all the glory of his wisdom, was unable to solve the mystery, though the fact is so common.

An egg is transformed into a bird or a fowl with body, wings, limbs, and with a plumage all sparkling with gold and beauty. But *how?* And, in addition, life has been evolved where apparently there was no life. Is there anything connected with the facts of the resurrection *more* mysterious or *more* remarkable than we behold in *this* fact.

Light passes at the rate of two hundred thousand miles per second. This is a demonstrated fact in science. But who can explain either the phenomena of light or the process by which this astonishing feat is performed. In these chapters we have expressed the belief that the soul, in the celestial life, would possess the ability to range through the universe at will. Some are inclined to ridicule this thought as an *impossibility*. But what is there connected with the supposition *more* impossible than the well-known fact just now stated with regard to light?

Again: the sunlight comes to our earth, a distance of ninety-two millions of miles in the space of seven minutes. It darts from world to world, through the universe, with the same inconceivable velocity; and yet, what is among the most astonishing facts in nature, it falls so softly and so gently upon the earth as not to stir the smallest leaf or disturb the most delicate flower, but instead it is through its silent influence, vitality and strength are afforded these things. And equally remarkable is the fact, that, though its rays are resisted by some of the softer materials and cannot pass beyond them, it penetrates some of the hardest without hindrance. Place a board in the sun's rays and they are obstructed. Remove the board and place in its stead a thick plate of glass, and though its pores are a thousand times more compact, they pierce it without hindrance. They will even dance and play in a diamond, the hardest known substance, with the same case and readiness with which they penetrate a fountain of limpid water.

These are *facts* which no intelligent man or woman will deny; and yet if we had never witnessed them, so wonderful are they, we should be inclined to say they are *impossible,* or pronounce them *miracles ;* and yet they are simple developments of the forces inherent in nature which regulate and control the outward universe. *Now we ask nothing more impossible for the soul than is* THUS GRANTED TO MATTER. If the sun's rays pass with such incredible velocity, and yet never disturb the most delicate thing with which they come in contact ;—if they are capable of penetrating the hardest substances without hindrance or without derangement of their own organism, what is there so hard of belief in the supposition that the immortal spirit of man,—by which we mean the *man himself,*—shall possess, at least, *equal* ability to perform the same wonders? The rays of the sun traverse millions of miles of space as quick as thought. Why not your disembodied spirit? These rays penetrate your windows and enter your room, enrobing all things there with the glory of their presence ! Why cannot your risen friend come into your room, if desirous of doing so, through the same medium, bringing equal joy to your heart ? Why should we limit the powers of the human soul,—*that* being really the most mysterious, wonderful and divine of all things in the universe, so far as we know, and still concede to the grosser material of nature the most astonishing ability and capacity? Can the man who has no faith in a hereafter, no belief in the existence of a world of spirits or that there can be such a place or state as heaven, give any reasonable answer to this question? To our mind there is nothing too good, too wonderful, too glorious, to be the gift of infinite wisdom and power, when controlled by infinite goodness. Hence we believe in a glorious hereafter for all God's children!

The same wonders are connected with electricity. Fifty years ago, the idea would have been treated with ridicule, that thousands of miles of space could be practically annihilated between two friends so that the one could sit in his office in Boston, and the other in his in London or St. Petersburg, and converse together as if face to face, without the least hindrance or the loss of a moment's time. And yet this is often done. Two persons within the sound of each other's voices in an ordinary room, do not communicate with each other more rapidly, or feel that they are in nearer proximity to each other, than do those who are thus conversing through a space of several thousand miles. They will laugh over each other's sayings as if really in each other's presence; give the salutations of the day, "Good morning to you," or "good evening," and take their leave of each other when going out on business, or to dine, or to call on a friend, as if personally present with each other. This is all true as a development in science. Nobody denies it; and as astonishing as it is, it is now scarcely regarded as a wonder, so soon do we become habituated to what we know to be true in philosophy.

Cannot the reader see by the exhibition of this fact, how, in some manner we do not now comprehend, space is annihilated with God and may be with us in the hereafter? There is, then, nothing unnatural or far-fetched in the supposition that when the soul has passed through the process of the resurrection, and been brought into a more ethereal sphere; —when "this corruptible shall have put on incorruption, and this mortal shall have put on immortality," and we shall have emerged from the dust and clogs of the earthy, we can pass like an angel, with the sun-beams, or the electric agent, from world to world, through infinity of space! How grand the thought, and how in harmony with the nature of that great and good Being who has created all things to confer happiness upon all! Surely there is a home in heaven for the wandering and weary of earth's children. Let us have faith in this comforting truth and say with the apostle that "the sufferings of this present time are not worthy to be compared to the glory that shall be revealed in us."

> "No mortal eye hath seen
>   The glories of that land beyond the river,
> Its crystal lakes, its fields of living green,
> Its fadeless flowers and the unchanging sheen,
>   Around the throne forever.
>
> "Ear hath not heard the song
>   Of rapturous praise within that shining portal;
> No heart of man hath dreamed what joys belong
> To that redeemed and happy blood-washed **throng**,
>   All glorious and immortal!"

CHAPTER VII.

The Death of the Body no Proof of the Destruction of the Soul.

Nothing in Nature is ever absolutely Destroyed.—Changes by Fire, Flood, Death and universal Decomposition are continually taking place, but change never necessarily implies Destruction.—Vegetation is constantly springing into Existence and falling to Decay, but not a particle of its Substance is lost.—Nor is it possible to destroy the inward Forces which control matter.—If then the absolute Destruction of the Body is impossible, is it probable the divine Essence of the Soul Perishes?—Facts adduced.

HAVING thus explained our conception of what the resurrection is, in a manner so simple that all can comprehend us, we wish now, once again, to ask the candid reader what there is still left as a stumbling block in the way of his faith?

He may answer that the idea is incomprehensible to him and therefore beyond his belief, "that the soul can retain its organism and consciousness after the brain, through which it acts in conjunction with the body, has been destroyed. When the body ceases to be, then the soul must cease to be."

But can the body cease to be? Is it possible, by any methods known to the human mind, to destroy absolutely man's physical being or any part of it? Can the most minute particle of matter be annihilated?—so much as a grain of sand, or spire of grass, or bit of wood? Science answers these questions with a positive negative. Change of form may transpire, as it is perpetually transpiring in the elements of nature, but this is all. Nothing is destroyed. The element of fire produces change. A whole city is devoured in a night, but not a particle of it is annihilated. Matter is perpetually shifting from place to place. The earth is visited by floods, which are succeeded by droughts, but not a particle of matter is added to or subtracted from the universe in consequence. The hardest substances are converted into gaseous vapor, and then resolved into their original condition. The human body decomposes after death, and is combined in new organisms. Nothing absolutely perishes. Now if the body, the grosser material, never ceases to exist, is it reasonable to suppose that the reasoning, God-like principle can perish?

But further. We have spoken of the unseen forces in nature which are supposed to be combined with electricity, magnetism, heat, etc., and which are in perpetual operation producing the changes which are observable in the outer world. Philosophers call them "subtile essences which elude our dull and blunt senses." In this particular they are analogous to the soul. Indeed, they are the soul of nature, and we *know* they exist as certainly as we know the outward elements of nature exist, for every moment we behold their *effects*.

When we look upon the springing corn, the blooming tree, the ripening fruit, we know that *there are forces in nature to produce these results*. When we behold the wonderful exhibitions of the human mind which are everywhere displayed in civilized life, we know that man must be in possession of a soul, though of its form and essence we know nothing. Now the truth we wish to impress upon the mind of the skeptic in connection with this subject, *is this*, that not only is *matter* indestructible, but also the *inward forces* which are the *soul of nature*. Produce whatever change you will in the outward world, yet the inward forces of which we speak still remain. As an illustration: electricity gathers in the threatening cloud and darts along the sky or seeks equilibrium by dashing to earth, carrying destruction in its line and producing violent changes in the physical world. But is one particle of the electrical agent thereby destroyed? By no means. It has only assumed a new position or taken a new form.

Take another example: that of the growth of vegetation. Trees, plants, grass and flowers are constantly springing into existence through the action of the hidden forces which we have described. Now the destruction of everything which proceeds from the earth in the vegetable world, will have no effect on these forces. Earthquakes, fire or other causes may produce changes in the face of nature, but in no possible manner can the subtile agencies which lie within and are the soul of nature, be annihilated. The main argument with the materialist is, that the soul cannot survive the dissolution of the body. But instead of this, nature and science combine in maintaining the sublime, Christian doctrine of immortality. The analogies we have presented, afford us not the shadow of a reason to imagine that the more subtile element of the soul can be destroyed by the dissolution of the body. Take nature in the rough; cut down the forest; turn up the stumps; burn the locality all over, and break up and overturn the soil to such an extent as to utterly change its outward appearance so that no one would recognize it, and cast in the seed and how soon you will discover the subtile forces of nature there still, all in activity, producing a resurrection grand and wonderful.

Or take a bar of iron, place it in a forge and heat it until it becomes white, sparkling, and as the blacksmith would say, all "alive" with the glowing element. Remove it from the furnace and it soon becomes black, and, in appearance, *dead* again. Where is the heat or life which but a moment ago was so visible to the senses? Is it affirmed to be annihilated because it is no longer combined with the iron? This would be just as reasonable as to contend that the soul of your friend is not in existence because his body lies before you cold in death. The heat has gone out of the iron, and become imperceptible to the sense of vision and of touch, but it is just as really in existence as when combined with the iron. If a heated iron is immersed in water, the heat immediately escapes from the iron, generates steam, combines with it, and so passes off into the atmosphere. Not a particle of it is lost. Why is it not just as reasonable to suppose that when the human body is being divested of its vitality and passing through the process of dying, then the soul, the immortal essence, the image of the heavenly, leaves its earthy tenement and is clothed upon with its pure, ethereal body, and so passes into a higher, more refined and glorified form of spiritual existence?

Thus it will be seen that all around us in nature exist facts analogous to those involved in the process of the resurrection. Multitudes of changes and combinations are perpetually taking place, which we can neither see nor comprehend, but the facts of which it would be folly for us to deny. What we need is FAITH. Faith in God, in the pure and beautiful and eternal. We have not offered these illustrations so much to prove another and diviner life, as to show that nature confirms our faith in such an existence. The New Testament is the fountain whence we draw truth and inspiration on this great question, but it is pleasing and hopeful to know that the voice of God in nature, and the voice of God through Christ and his apostles, are one and the same voice. Progress is a law of our spiritual being. Nature never opposes this truth but strengthens it by a thousand analogies. How many things there are in the visible world around us under the influence of the same law.

"It is one of the most interesting studies in natural science," says an eminent naturalist, "to trace the same living being as it is manifested in different and successive forms. Science describes insects, which, in different stages of being, live in different elements. At first, perhaps an individual of this class lives in the water,—a mere worm; its whole organization adapted to that state, and dying if taken from it. At length it passes through a dormant condition resembling death, during which this organization is thrown off, when it bursts forth in a totally different form, with new organs and new sensations, and emerges from the water, to dart, a winged thing, through the air, with powers adapted to its new organization and new condition of existence."

If all this now is true of an insect,—a little, unsightly worm, that, as we have seen, though in possession of no reasoning mind, no hope, no desire, no divine aspirations, is yet transformed into a being so wonderfully gorgeous that the little child cries out with astonished delight on beholding it,—why should it not be of man, who is the noblest work of God; who dreads death more than all things, and who feels that if the grave ends his being, his existence in this world seems without aim or design, and a total failure, and that the great and good God has given him lofty desires, ardent hopes and divine and noble aspirations only to be crushed and annihilated in the dust and rubbish of the grave?

Oh, dear reader, this cannot be! Thanks to God, it cannot be!

"We are passing away, passing away,"

it is true. Dear ones are going from us, and yet it may be not so far from us, but that with their increased capacity, they may know of our condition and can return to us instantly at will and be around and about us to guard and bless us. The thought is a beautiful one and comforting as beautiful; and it may be so:—

"We know that in day-time,
There are stars about us just as at night,
Though to our dim sight invisible;
So to a spirit all heaven may be as full
Of spirits, as a beam of light of moats!"

Let us then have hope in the spiritual which is the real of our being. Let us live every day of our existence as if holding a sacred relation to the hereafter and the dear ones who have entered there, and a sacred nearness to them, cherishing in our hearts the glorious sentiment of the apostle, who saw the future, and even felt it already within his grasp, as he exclaimed, "We do know that if this earthly house of our tabernacle were dissolved, *we* have a building of God, an house not made with hands eternal in the heavens;" or when, with his soul full of enthusiasm and gratitude, he exclaimed, "I am persuaded that neither DEATH, nor life, nor angels, nor principalities, nor powers, nor things present, nor things to come, nor height, nor depth, nor any other creature shall be able to separate us from the love of God, which is in Christ Jesus our Lord." Death then will not separate us from God's love, which demonstrates that we shall live again. If annihilated how could we continue to be the objects of the divine affection! Thanks to God, heaven is the home of the soul,—yea, the home of *all* souls!

> "Beyond life's toils and cares,
>   Its hopes and joys, its weariness and sorrow,
>   Its sleepless nights, its days of smiles and tears,
>   Will be a long, sweet life, unmarked by years,
>   One bright, unending morrow.
>
> Beyond time's troubled stream,
>   Beyond the chilling waves of death's dark river,
>   Beyond life's lowering clouds and fitful gleams,
>   Its dark realities and brighter dreams,
>   A beautiful forever!"

Oh, if you believe this, and feel it in your soul, you can triumph over the thought of death. For you death shall have no terrors. And when your dear ones are taken from you and you feel yourself a sad and unhappy mourner, you can lift up the sublime prayer of the ancient servant of God, when he exclaimed, "All thy waves and thy billows have gone over me, *yet* the Lord will command his loving kindness in the day-time, and in the night his song shall be with me. Why art thou cast down, O my soul? and why art thou disquieted within me? Hope thou in God, for I shall yet praise Him, who is the health of my countenance and my God!"

CHAPTER VIII.

The Soul's Triumph over the Body.

The main argument of the Materialist considered.—No man knows or can prove that the Soul Perishes on the Death and Dissolution of the Body.—Thousands have testified that they have seen and conversed with their Departed Friends.—Interesting Facts.—Testimony of Medical Men.—Dr. Kane's assertion.—Apparent Death of a Clergyman.—What he Saw and Heard.—Interesting Facts.—The Soul's Triumph over the Body in Death.

WE have already considered the question of our correspondent, "Is there another life?" at much greater length than we contemplated when we began; but in justice to our subject and to our own feelings, we cannot take leave of it, till we have offered a few facts of a different nature from those already adduced, in answer to the argument of the materialist that the soul cannot retain its organism and its consciousness after the brain, through which it acts in conjunction with the body, has been destroyed. Upon this assertion is based the main argument of the class of men who deny the doctrine of immortality. They say that the soul is entirely dependent upon the body for its existence; —that the brain is not only essential, but indispensable to all mental operations; that the strength of the mental faculties depends wholly upon the strength of the physical brain, and that, therefore, when the body becomes weakened by disease, and fades away more and more till death ensues, the mental powers in like manner lose their vigor, become correspondingly debilitated, and, at length, incapacitated for thought and all consciousness, perish totally on the death of the body.

But all this is mere assumption utterly destitute of *proof*. Who *knows* that the soul cannot retain its organization and consciousness after the death and dissolution of the body? Or that it perishes utterly on the death of the body? If the reader will reflect, he will see that three out of the four above assertions of the materialist are just what no man can know, or possibly prove. How can we know or prove that the human soul at death becomes a *nonentity?* This is impossible; for it is impossible to see, or feel, or discover what *does not exist*, or to know anything about it. While, on the other hand, hundreds and thousands of people have testified in words most sincere and earnest that they KNEW disembodied spirits existed for they had often seen them and conversed with them. This is the positive declaration of many of God's servants, chosen to bear His truth to the nations, as recorded in the Bible. In all ages, and among nearly all people who have lived upon earth, have these sentiments prevailed, and these facts been asserted. Not only the ignorant, but the educated have testified to the same truth. Emanuel Swedenborg founds his whole system of religion and the **existence of spirits** in the other life mainly on what he professed to *have seen*, and felt, while very many people in all parts of Christendom, among whom were men and women of unquestioned intelligence and veracity, have had their souls filled with delight at the spiritual presence, from time to time, of some dear one gone. It is no uncommon thing for persons dying to describe in the most glowing terms, what they see as they look into the glorious vista that opens before them. Father, mother, husband or wife or loved children who had passed away, perhaps months or years before, were around them looking upon them with sweetest faces, and clad in robes of celestial brightness and beauty and waiting the liberation of their own souls, and their full entrance into the divine and spiritual. This is what a vast multitude have testified to, and so certain have they been of the truth of what they affirmed that it was impossible to shake their faith in its reality. They could see their departed friends as plainly as they ever saw them while in the flesh and they *knew* whereof they affirmed. It was not a matter concerning which there was any question in their minds. We have attended the funeral of a score or more of persons who, in their last moments, were permitted to gaze upon these ravishing, celestial scenes. One, a young lady, who saw her father and sister, and her betrothed who died a few weeks before their marriage was to have been consummated. Oh, what joy did she express at the sight. Another,—a young man,—a relative by marriage, who was sick six months in our family. When he drew near his earthly end he was certain he saw his mother who had died a few years before. She looked upon him with the sweetest expression and he felt her take hold of his arm, precisely as she did when he was a boy. No one could convince him that all this was not reality.

During our experience of sixteen years as editor of a religious paper, we have published many obituaries of persons, younger and older, who in their last hours bore enrapturing testimony to facts of the same general character.

Now, is all this hallucination and deception? Have the thousands since the beginning of the world, who rejoiced in the happy belief that they had seen and conversed with the disembodied spirits of kindred and friends, been utterly mistaken? Are we to have no confidence in the recorded facts and teachings of the Bible? If the assertion of the materialist,—that the soul cannot survive the death and dissolution of the body is true, then these questions must be answered in a way to give the lie to all we have described and to every pretension that the spirit of any man or woman has been seen, or ever existed after death, since the beginning of the world,—an alternative we cannot say we are prepared to adopt. For, though we have never seen a spirit, and though we have stated in these pages that the spiritual, under ordinary conditions, cannot be seen with our mortal vision, still we should not dare assert that the declarations of so many thousands of intelligent men and women, testifying to what they had seen, were all false. We believe that the mind, when in a certain abnormal state, can see and hear what persons in a normal condition cannot see and hear. In former years, when familiar with the practice of Mesmerism, the subject, when under magnetic influence and blind-folded, would describe accurately all that was said and done in another room, or in another dwelling two squares distant, when neither ourself nor any person present had any knowledge of the facts till thus revealed. The person entranced seemed in some incomprehensible manner, *independent of the outward senses*, to see and hear all that was done as if absolutely present.

So we believe it often is when death approaches, and at other times, with the mind in certain exalted conditions. It sees and hears what others present cannot see and hear. Above and all around may be a halo of glory to that soul. The most enchanting scenes may be open to its gaze, and the most enrapturing strains of celestial harmony may be wafted to its spiritual senses, while those who stand weeping around, or filled with astonished delight as they listen to the rapturous expressions coming from dying lips, may see and hear nothing.

We do not say that we *know* all this to be true; but we do say we *believe* it ; and, further, that there is nothing more extraordinary or impossible about it than we find connected with the well-known fact just now mentioned,—that when the senses are under the influence of magnetism, the soul can see and hear what is transpiring at a distance, and what no person present, not in the same mental condition, can possibly see or hear or know anything about.

And thus, all these considerations, based upon the declarations of many thousands of good Christians, are so much proof to our mind, that the soul can and does survive the death and dissolution of the body; while the materialist can furnish no proof in favor of his positive assertion that the soul perishes on the death of the body.

But there are other considerations which we are anxious to present, showing the palpable error of the statement that the vigor and integrity of the soul depend upon the health and vigor of the body. There never was a greater mistake. It is true that *sometimes* mental debility is manifested in consequence of physical debility; but in order for the argument of the materialist to weigh anything with the intelligent mind, it must be shown that the fact mentioned is the *invariable result of physical debility*. Instead of this being true, every well-informed, experienced, medical practitioner will testify to the fact that in many cases the debility of the body in consequence of sickness or accident, has no weakening effect at all upon the mind, but instead, serves only to render it the more vigorous and brilliant. To employ the language of another, who has given the subject much study and thought: "Not only may the limbs be amputated, the eyes quenched, the lungs almost consumed, but the nerves may be paralyzed, the brain wounded or diseased, and yet the mind may remain unimpaired, the soul unclouded, nay, as if in mockery of mere physical hindrances, the spirit may wield a mightier power and wing a loftier flight than ever before." This is true. But how can it be true if the soul is the result of physical organization,—is dependent upon it for its condition of vitality and vigor and gradually perishes with the debility and death of the body?

We recollect, years ago, being at the home of an intelligent medical gentleman * of extensive practice, when he returned from a professional visit to a patient. He said, with much animation, that within the past two days he had witnessed an exhibition of mental vigor in an attenuated, and what he had regarded as a dying frame, which had served to convince him more than all the books he had ever read, of the truth that the soul was superior to the body, could triumph over it, and live independent of it. He then went on, in his calm, thoughtful, intelligent way, while tears glistened in his eyes, to tell us, in touching words, of a widow woman, the mother of eight children, to whom he was called three weeks before, and whom he had found very sick with fever. She was poor, but intelligent, and having so large a family of children all dependent on her under God for their daily bread, she had

---
* Dr. Benjamin Bradford of Livermore, Maine.

not sent for him, for fear of expense, till she was far on the road to death. "From the first," he said, "I had no hope she would recover. The most alarming symptoms I have ever witnessed in one sick with the same disease made their appearance, and indicated, in my apprehension, certain death. All the time, contrary to what is often the case, her mind has been clear and strong, and when she saw by my appearance that I thought she would not live, she said, 'Doctor, I MUST LIVE. *Think of my eight children. I cannot die and leave them to the charities of a cold world.*'

"I quieted and comforted her as well as I could by saying that she must keep up good heart, and hope for the best, and leave the rest with One who knows better than we what to do for us. But this was said without heart, for every symptom I could discover indicated only death. All other patients I have ever seen with similar developments have died, and yet *this woman is alive and will recover. The vigor of her soul has saved her body from the grave!* This is what I am convinced of," said the old gentleman, as tears stood in his eyes. "There is not an organ in her body, nor any part of her physical being, however minute, but what is diseased. Her brain has been apparently all on fire for days, and yet through the whole, her mind has been entirely unclouded and never before manifested such thought and vigor. She continued to say that she could not die and leave her dear children; and, finally, she said she *must* not, and *would* not! Thus spoke and thus looked her *soul* when every symptom of her body indicated impending dissolution. Her soul seemed to be independent of her body and yet to have control of it, and to conquer the disease by the will just as a man can conquer and control a passion by the force of the will; all of which demonstrates the falsity of the statement that the soul receives its vitality and energy from the vitality and energy of the body."

Multitudes of instances are on record which might be adduced in proof of the same fact. Dr. Kane once said :—"Tell about the influence of the body over the soul; why, I have seen enough to convince me that the soul can lift the body out of its boots." This declaration is more expressive than elegant, but he gives the following striking instance in proof of his assertion :—

"When our Captain was dying,—I say *dying*, for I have seen scurvy enough to know,—I never saw a case so bad that either lived or died;—men usually die before they are as ill as he was;—there was trouble on board, and there might be mutiny, and I felt that he owed even the repose of dying to the service. So I went to his bunk and shouted in his ear, 'Mutiny! Captain, mutiny!' He shook off the cadaveric stupor. 'Set me up,' said he, 'and order those fellows before me!' He heard their complaint, ordered punishment, and from that hour convalesced."

His biographer* might well call this "a pearl." The strong will of the dying man triumphed even when his body showed every outward sign of impending dissolution.

Then again the very curious and mysterious phenomena of sleep which no mind has ever fully understood, show how active is the soul when all the outward senses are closed and benumbed as if unconscious in death. It is contended by those who have given the subject the most careful attention that the soul never sleeps, but instead is often in a far more exalted condition than when the outward faculties are awake, reveling in philosophy, poetry, and even solving the most difficult problems in mathematics. How can all this be if the brain is a *sine qua non* to thought, reflection, calculation, reason?

Another consideration which has great weight with us as proof that the soul can and will retain its consciousness, after death, is the fact that in many well authenticated instances, persons, to all outward appearance, have died;—no movement of the heart or lungs was detected,—all sensation and consciousness for days seemed suspended, during which the body was pale and cold and seemingly lifeless;—and yet all the while the soul, though apparently absent from the body, not only retained its consciousness, but in some instances experienced the most wonderful increase of mental ability. A case

---

* Biography of Elisha Kent Kane, by William Elder, pp 251-252.

of this kind transpired some years ago in Kentucky, where a young lady, who had been in a somewhat singular condition of health for a month, was found apparently dead on her bed one summer afternoon. A physician was called, who, after proper examination, said the vital spark had fled, and preparations were accordingly made for her funeral. In the morning of the third day after, before the service was to be performed in the afternoon, the mother, whose soul was bowed in grief, thought she discovered that the cheeks of her daughter were slightly tinged with a hectic flush, on which she began to feel that her child might not, after all, be dead. Another physician was immediately summoned, and after many appliances, and much external friction by rubbing, "she that was dead" suddenly opened her eyes and in a little while sat up in bed, and began to talk in her common tones, and soon appeared as if in her ordinary condition of health. But her soul was in ecstasy at what she had seen and heard during her absence from the body, for that she had been out of the body and was only connected with it by the most attenuated thread, she was certain. She described the scenery of the celestial world and repeated poetry, beautiful and sublime, which she was never known to rehearse before and which she had no ability to produce when in her normal condition. All of which produced great excitement among the people of that section.

Another somewhat similar case was that of William Tennant, a Presbyterian clergyman of the last century.

"While pursuing his theological studies his health became seriously impaired, and he was troubled with great and distressing doubts concerning his spiritual condition, when, as he was conversing with his brother one morning about the state of his soul, he suddenly seemed to expire. The usual preparations were made for the funeral, and the friends and neighbors were invited to attend it the next day. But in the evening, a young physician, his intimate friend, detected, as he thought, some signs of life; and by urgent entreaty he caused the burial to be deferred till the third day, and then, when the friends and physician, who had not ceased to use all possible means of resuscitation, were on the point of giving up the case in despair, suddenly the patient opened his eyes, groaned, and fainted.

"For a long time he seemed to hang midway between life and death, but at last he fully recovered his health of body and his powers of mind; and afterwards he gave to a friend, who published it, an account of what he had experienced in his wondrous trance. He said that while conversing with his brother, he suddenly found himself in another state of existence, and under the direction of some superior being, who conducted him through the aerial regions till he beheld an ineffable glory, and a great multitude, singing and rejoicing in a manner impossible to describe; but when he expressed a wish to join the happy throng, he was told that he must return to earth. Grieving that it must be so, he awoke and saw his brother standing by him, reasoning with the physician about his condition, whether he were really dead or yet alive. It seemed to him but a few moments that he had been absent from the body, but in that little space of time, he had seen and heard, or thought, what left a deep and lasting impression on his mind. In his account of it he said, 'The ravishing songs and hallelujahs that I heard, and the very words that were uttered, were not out of my ears, when awake, for at least three years.' We may not be able to give any satisfactory explanation of these facts, but of the facts themselves, the facts that he fell into such a trance, that after three days he recovered from it, and that he gave this account of what had passed, or seemed to have passed, in his mind during that time, there can be no doubt. And if in such a case the soul can act with such amazing energy, while the body is utterly insensible and motionless, as if dead, why may it not survive and act, when the body is actually dead, dissolved in dust, and thrown off like an encumbering weight or garment, which the runner in a race throws off lest it should hinder his swift progress towards the goal?" *

But what to *our* mind is stronger evidence of immortality than all else, and more prophetic of a

---
* From the "Christian Doctrine of the Soul," by H. C. Estes, D. D.

home in heaven for the soul, is the wonderful phenomena often witnessed up to the very moment of dissolution and the perfect triumph of the soul over death and all that could stand between it and heaven. We have briefly referred to this fact before in these pages, but its importance demands a more extended notice ere we conclude what we have to offer on the question of our correspondent, "Is there a Future Life for man?"

We employ the language of a clergyman * of culture, experience and deep religious feeling, in describing what we have repeatedly witnessed at the bed-side of the dying. We do it to strengthen our testimony by that of another. He says:—

"I have repeatedly stood by the death-bed of one attenuated by long infirmity, every vital process clogged, the pulse intermittent, the blood already becoming stagnant; and I have seen the dying still in the vigor of his intellect, master of his position, clearer and stronger in thought and judgment than any one of the by-standers, addressing appropriate counsel or consolation to each of the afflicted circle, dictating messages of love to the absent, and leaving no person or interest forgotten that had the remotest right to a place in his remembrance. I have heard, too, in the hour and in the embrace of death, not the feverish ecstasies of unreasoning fanaticism, but the serene utterances of a mature religious wis-

---

* A. P. Peabody, D. D., LL.D. in his "Christianity the Religion of Nature," pp 184-185.

dom, of undoubting faith, of quiet trust, of a foreseeing hope that had already crossed the separating stream, and passed within the golden gates; and in the eye kindled with a purer, holier light than ever glows except in the Christian's ascension-room, in the wan countenance radiant with the foreshining of the heavenly day, in the air of joyous expectancy with which the parting moment is waited for and welcomed, the soul's voice is: 'Death, I am not thine, and I defy thy power. I am mightier than thou art. Thou art but the door-keeper of my house not made with hands, my usher through the resurrection into the blessed society of the unfallen and the redeemed.' From such a death-scene into annihilation how vast the leap! between them how immeasurable the contrast! while there seems not a step, not even a filmy cloud or an unparted veil, between the scene and heaven."

The truth of all this is indelibly enstamped upon our own soul by what we have personally witnessed at the bed-side of the dying, the circumstances of a single case of which we feel that we must relate in these pages, notwithstanding their nearness to our own heart and home, and the great grief and sweet tenderness their relation must vividly recall. Though many dear friends were acquainted with all the facts of the case when they transpired, and though they many times urged us to make them public, we have never before felt that we could do so. And now it is only the hope that their relation may be the means of illuming some dark soul with faith in another life, or of comforting some saddened heart by inspiring it with the truth that dear ones gone are still living, and that they shall go to them and know them and live again in a world of beauty and blessedness, that induces us to speak out of our full heart what is so sacredly treasured there.

It was in the year 1860, that one with whom I had lived for more than twenty years in closest conjugal intimacy, passed into the better life, leaving an infant child but seven days old, besides three other dear children.* The last days of her life were attended with intense suffering, and yet nothing could exceed the calmness of her soul. She had been called to part, from time to time, with children, till five had preceded her to their heavenly home, one of whom,—"Charlie," the older, nearly four years old when he died,—was a very beautiful and promising child. Now the mother was to follow. On the night preceding her death as she obtained no rest, she requested me to lie down by her side and said if all were quiet she might fall into a drowse. It was probably twelve o'clock. The room was above stairs. It was in the month of February, and a moderate wood fire burned in the open fire-place. Just beyond the foot of the bed, the door opened into a hall which was lighted by a lamp upon a stand, placed but a short distance from the door,

---

* I was then Pastor of the Parish in Middletown, Conn., where the events here described transpired.

which, at the hour to which I refer, stood ajar perhaps six or eight inches, for the purpose of ventilation. As one reposed upon the bed, he could look directly through the aperture, formed by the door partially opened, into the hall beyond and see very distinctly what was there. I had lain there perhaps ten minutes during which I had whispered some words of encouragement to her, when she requested the nurse, who was sitting by the fire-side, to open the door. The nurse complied with her request, and the light in the hall shone into the room. In a short time she requested her to place the door as before. Then, after a few minutes, she asked her to open it again; then, soon she again requested her to close it. This she did three times, which somewhat alarmed both the nurse and myself for it indicated, as I thought, mental aberration; after which she lay a few minutes as if in deep thought, when she said, "I now *know* I am going to leave you and the dear children. I shall go to-morrow."

I was in great distress and begged of her not to talk in this way,—she would "be better in the morning." "No, not in the *morning*, but in the *evening* of to-morrow I shall be better," she replied. "Charlie has come for me and I *know* that I am going. But don't let it grieve or distress you, my husband, for it is the will of God, and whatever is *His* will must be for the best."

She seemed so calm and self-possessed and so

positive in her convictions,—as if she had certain knowledge of what would transpire,—that I was filled with alarm and grief, and asked her what had occurred to inspire her with such dreadful forebodings?

She said she saw nothing "dreadful" in what was before her. With the exception of the separation from those on earth so dear to her, all was bright and beautiful. "Charlie has come for me."

I asked her what she could mean by this,—for she was no believer in spiritualism, nor was she the least credulous or superstitious, but a clear-minded, excellent, sincere, Bible Christian, possessing the strongest possible faith in God and hope of heaven.

She went on to say, in touching tones, that as soon as I had lain down beside her, Charlie appeared in the hall and looked in upon her through the aperture formed by the door standing a little ajar, as described above. She saw him by the full light of the hall lamp. He was nearly as high as the ceiling, and seemed clad in celestial light, with his face radiant with beauty,—the shining curls, glowing cheeks and large expressive eyes, she saw just as vividly as when he was in the flesh. "He looked charmingly attractive," she said, "and putting up his little hand in this way,"—and she described how with her own hand already as white as alabaster,—"and with his finger so ethereal, he beckoned me in this way,"—beckoning herself,—"to come with him, and smiled so sweetly! The scene was so enchanting, I could not speak, but could only gaze upon it! At length, I asked to have the door fully opened to see if the vision would remain; but as the door opened it departed. Then I asked to have the door closed as before, and to my joy the vision returned as before, with the same celestial radiance, the same angelic sweetness. When the door was opened again, again it vanished, and after the third time, it came no more. It will not come again. Ah, no! but I shall go to the bright world radiant with spiritual beauty, and join the glad throng among whom are all the dear ones gone. Who knows but I am needed there? Our family above is larger than our family here, you know."

From this time till the moment of her death, which transpired at seven o'clock the next evening, she seemed to rise entirely out of and above the conditions which surrounded her. Her body was dying, and yet to *her* there was no death. She saw not the grave, but only her risen Saviour and the delights and glories of the heavenly world. She slept a little that night but in the morning her soul was all alive to the interests and happiness of those she was so soon to leave. When her physicians came, at her request to tell her the plain truth, they said they could afford no hope, and when they listened to her calm, loving words, so full of resignation and trust, they were affected to tears. She had her person and room put in condition to afford the most cheerful aspect, as if there was to be no *death* there, but only a *resurrection;* that she was to put off her mortal garment for her ascension robe. She had the children brought to her bed-side and sing the charming hymns she had taught them, about heaven and the angels, and gave them wise and loving counsel; talked to them of the sweet home in heaven, to which she was going where she would meet their little brothers, * and where she would again live with them. All present, with the exception of herself, were melted to tears. To her all was serenity and holy reconciliation and joy.

Then she sent word to some of her most intimate parish friends that she was about to leave them for the last time, and would be very glad to see them and bid them good-by; and they came,—for she was a dear friend to many of them,—and entered her room so sad in appearance, as if it were a funeral; but as they witnessed her perfect triumph over the grave,—noticed her countenance illumined with the bright hope of heaven, and listened to her sweetly-chosen words that were "like apples of gold in pictures of silver," so full of peace and spiritual joy,—their sadness was dissipated, the room seemed filled with glory, and they returned to their homes with all unbelief with reference to a future life banished, and their souls filled with a serene joy, and a perfect trust in the goodness of God and hope of heaven.

---

* All of the five children whom God had called to Himself were boys.

By those who called, she sent affectionate words to others, asking them also to come and see her, so that during the day nearly a hundred were at her bedside. All this time, it will be remembered, she was dying, and yet triumphing over her pains and the thought of death and the grave. At one time when the room was nearly full, one Brother present said, "Mrs. Q., I greatly fear so many being here at a time will distress you;" to which she instantly replied, "Oh, no, Brother Stearns, I am beyond all distress of either body or soul. Nothing can disturb me now." And thus she continued all day, seeing her friends, for every one of whom she had some kind, sweet word, till she gently fell asleep in Jesus, who appeared very near to her at that moment. She grew weaker and weaker in body, but in her soul stronger and stronger. She closed her eyes, but whispered that when she was going she would press my hand. For a half hour there was no motion of a limb or muscle, and no one knew or could tell whether she was "in the body or out." Suddenly a slight pressure of the hand was felt, she relaxed her hold, brought a little sigh, and was gone.

Could this be *death to that soul?* It was impossible for me to *feel* it so. From such a scene "into annihilation how vast the leap." "Between them how immeasurable the contrast;" while there appeared "not a step, not even a filmy cloud between her exalted soul and heaven." All present, whatever their religious views, testified as one person that to *her* there was no death. From that day to the present I can never think of her in connection with the corruption of the grave, but only as being in heaven, incorruptible, spiritual and glorious. And, I repeat, this strength and exaltation of the soul, and other wonderful phenomena, manifested when the bodily form is attenuated by disease, is more prophetic of immortality, and more convincing proof, to my mind, of another existence for the soul, than all other considerations. Most emphatically do I feel to respond to the truthful sentiment of the poet:—

> "There is no death! What seems so is transition;
> This life of mortal breath
> Is but a suburb of the life elysian,
> Whose portal we call death."

Here, then, we conclude our reasons for our hope of another life. Others might be offered, but to our apprehension, they are of minor consideration. Those we have presented, to our mind, are conclusive, and though they seem independent of revelation, are in harmony with it. Indeed, really, they are the offspring of Christian thought and culture, and will have greatest weight with those who look first to Christ for hope of immortality and confide in the hand that lifted the widow's son from the bier, and in the voice that called Lazarus from the tomb. We know "He is the Resurrection and the Life," "Lord, to whom shall we go? Thou hast the words of eternal life." And yet, we trust our utterances in these pages, founded on the facts of science and the nature of the soul, will serve to strengthen the faith of the doubting in the declarations of Christ and the apostles concerning another life and the soul's home in heaven. God be praised for these sublime truths. "In my Father's house there are many mansions. If it were not so I would have told you. I go to prepare a place for you; and if I go and prepare a place for you I will come again and receive you unto myself, *that where I am* THERE YE MAY BE ALSO." How blessed this promise! How glorious the consummation it anticipates! Dear reader, you may be overwhelmed in sorrow because of the death of some cherished idol,—a wife, or husband, or child, or father, or mother, or brother, or sister. But do not longer weep. These partings are inevitable. All must experience their full meaning:—

"Friend after friend departs;
Who hath not lost a friend?
There is no union here of hearts,
That finds not here an end.
Were this frail world our only rest,
Living or dying, none were blest."

But, thanks to God, this "frail world" is not "our *only* rest!" Indeed, there is but little rest in it:—

"There is a world above,
Where parting is unknown,
A whole eternity of love
And blessedness alone!
And faith beholds the dying here
Translated to that happier sphere!"

Your loved one, then, is not dead, but still lives in a world of spirituality and joy. He is lifted above the storms of sin, the ravages of death and the curse of pain. Can you desire his return to the earthy? "Ye shall go to him;" for heaven is the ultimate home of all God's great family. Oh!

> "*This* is the hope, the blissful hope,
> Which Jesus's grace hath given;
> The hope when days and years have past,
> We ALL shall meet in heaven!"

As it is the gift of God's pure "grace," *you* are entitled to it. Receive it, then, dear Brother, dear Sister;—cherish it in your souls; cultivate gratitude to God for it, and sweet peace and spiritual joy shall be the fruits of blessedness it shall yield to your souls!

CHAPTER IX.

The Question of No Moral Change by a Change of Worlds, considered.

The Errors that Prevail in the Church relative to the Resurrection.—If the common Notions are Correct, Heaven can be a place of Happiness to None.—Modified Views of Restorationists and some Universalists not Sustained by the New Testament.—Consideration of the Question, Is there any Moral Change in Man in consequence of a change of Worlds?—Interesting Facts stated.

WE have thus far labored to prove a future existence for man,—*all* men,—with what success the reader must judge. We have proceeded upon the hypothesis, which is fully established by the plain and positive declarations of the New Testament, that that existence will be a vast improvement on the present, *to all God's children*, and that, therefore, death and the resurrection and immortality will be a vast and *unspeakable blessing to them all.* Hence, the doctrine that declares this glorious truth, is a joy and comfort to all who believe it, as we have endeavored to show. But this is not the view of most Christians with reference to this subject. They talk of Heaven as the Home of man, and the Future Life as an unspeakable blessing, it is true, but when we go further and question them relative *to whom* heaven will prove a home and a blessing, and listen to the answer, our song of joy is instantly hushed in the soul, while from it comes a wail of anguish and despair. For while we are told that all sentient creatures will be raised to another existence and be rendered immortal in their nature, we are also told that such are the conditions of salvation, that only a mere remnant of the great family of man will gain entrance to heaven, while all the remainder will be disowned of God, banished from the world of light and love, and with a curse, sentenced to the realms of irretrievable and endless suffering; that parents and children,—husbands and wives,—brothers and sisters, and those who were the dearest and sweetest friends to each other while on earth, will be separated forever,—one portion of whom will be admitted to glory, while the other will sink to the realms of endless darkness! And this is their *Gospel* doctrine of the resurrection which Christ revealed as a joy to the world! This the character of the comfort with which they would bind up the broken in heart;—the balm of consolation for the souls of the millions lacerated by the bitter anguish of affliction!

But if all this be the truth of the Gospel, how can the resurrection and immortality, or the hope of them, prove a source of joy to *any*, either in this life or the next? Such a pretension is a burlesque on consistency, and a mockery to all the sensibilities of the soul; for, surely, *such* an immortality will only be an existence of wretchedness that shall be endless to those who are banished from the world of glory, while those who enter there can enjoy nothing if they fail to find the dear ones in the better world to whom their souls were knit while on earth by ties so sweet, so tender, so enduring! To them, Heaven can be no home of happiness, no condition of delight—such as we have endeavored to describe —if they know, as they surely must, that these dear ones are doomed to hell. Nor to any who are living, can this thought—if they believe it—afford one ray of joy;—nothing indeed, but lamentation and mourning! So that regarding the subject in this light, the resurrection and such an existence are a curse rather than a blessing to man. Far better would it have been for him and all concerned,—for time and eternity,—to sleep the cold, blank sleep of annihilation;—to feel and know that the grave ends all his sufferings and his enjoyments. For ourself, a thousand times should we prefer to sleep undisturbed the sleep of annihilation, than to awaken into another life only to enter on a condition of suffering, or to a knowledge of the sufferings of those dear to us. Hence, the Gospel can prove no gospel to us if it declares this awful doctrine, nor can Christ prove a blessing if he came to reveal Heaven as the home of only a part of the human race. God is the common Father of all His great family, and Heaven must be the home of all, or it will be impossible for it to prove a place of happiness to any. All are interlinked by ties of affection and sympathy that have their origin in the bosom of infinite love and embrace the world; and if we sever the tenth or ten thousandth link, alike we break the chain, and the strains of celestial joy, that would otherwise ring through Heaven, would be changed to wailings of grief and sadness.

We cannot, therefore, banish even one poor wanderer, however sin-scarred and ragged in this life, from that dear home of many mansions prepared for all God's great family in Heaven. We cannot, because we do not believe *Christ can* or that *God will.* This it will be our design to endeavor to show in what may follow. Some poor soul may peruse these pages who may be stricken with grief at the loss of some dear friend who may have died without what is regarded as a "suitable preparation" for death, and hence he may be filled with awful alarm and anxiety, lest in the resurrection, God in his wrath would doom him to hell. We wish to relieve all hearts of any such error and anguish, by showing that the true teaching of the resurrection as revealed in the New Testament, admits the truth of no such dreadful sentiment. But instead, reveals

"A blessed Home where ALL shall meet
And never, never part again;
Where those who loved on earth, repeat
The vows they pledged in sorrow then.

"In that bright home where earthly woe
And earthly sorrow, all shall cease;
No sin shall grieve, no tear shall flow,
For all shall dwell in love and peace!"

Then there are those who reject the above extreme

views respecting the wrath of God and the endlessness of suffering for a portion of God's great family in the resurrection life, but who, nevertheless, believe that the future is a world of sin and suffering as well as this; that a change of worlds works no moral change in man; that he carries all his evil lusts and passions with him into the resurrection life, and begins there where he leaves off here, and hence he will continue to be an object of God's displeasure and punishment there as well as here.

By reference to the extracts of letters from correspondents published in the first pages of this book, it will be seen that there are not a few who entertain these views. They ask us if we "believe there will be any moral change in man on his passing from this life into the next?" "Shall we not be sinners there as well as here?" "And if we sin there,—as we shall if we possess the same moral natures there as here,—shall we not be punished? But if we possess natures that will lead us to sin in the other life, *when* will our sinning cease and we become holy and happy?"

And these questions are asked by Universalist clergymen who say that their "minds are not entirely clear on these points;" all of which demonstrates not only the vagueness of the apprehensions which exist in the minds of thousands on this sublime and glorious theme, but that the above views are entertained by those even who believe in the *final* end of all sin and suffering and the *ultimate* restoration of all God's children to a blessed condition of holiness and happiness.

All this, though an unspeakable improvement upon the old ideas, detracts immensely from the beautiful doctrine of the Gospel relative to the resurrection and the resurrection life; robs Heaven of its glory and the soul of that sublime hope of the pure and beautiful, which is "an anchor of the soul sure and steadfast." If the above concerning the future life be true, then that life will be no improvement on the present, and, therefore, Heaven can be no HOME, such as the confiding Christian anticipates, for *any* of God's creatures, for no soul will be sinless there, or

"Nearer, my God, to Thee"

than in the present, imperfect life. Though translated from this existence to another, all souls will still be under the dominion of sin and therefore continue in a condition of pain and sorrow and error. For these views, the author of these chapters wishes to say distinctly, he has no sympathy; on the contrary, to behold the beautiful truths of the Gospel thus bereft of their sweetness and enshrouded in darkness in the house of its friends, is a source of unspeakable regret to him; hence he would give them no countenance, but employ his efforts, however limited, in their correction. Will the reader carefully peruse what we have to offer while we proceed to show that these ideas can have no foundation in fact nor in the divine Word? In doing this we shall endeavor to answer the questions of our correspondents:—

"*Do you believe there will be any moral change in man on his passing from this world into the next?*" "*Shall we not be the same beings in the resurrection life that we are in this?*"

The grounds that the supporters of what are called evangelical doctrines have taken against the beautiful truths taught in the Gospel as received by Universalists, is that *the soul is fitted in this life by regeneration* or the *new birth,*—wrought by the influence of the Holy Spirit,—for the purity and glory of Heaven. Hence they have denied the doctrine of any change in the moral and spiritual condition of the soul at the time of death or subsequently. In the resurrection, men and women, they contend, will possess precisely the same minds and the same moral character they possessed at the time of death. And, hence, they have quoted, times without number, to sustain their position, for Scripture what is not in the Bible. "As the tree falls in this world, so shall it lie in the next." And "as death leaves us so judgment will find us." "He that is filthy when God calls for him, must be filthy still, and he that is holy must be holy still." And thus have they taught that upon this basis God would make a distinction between the righteous and the wicked in the resurrection life, saving the former with an everlasting salvation, because they are suitably "prepared" for Heaven before death, but condemning the latter to punishment that shall never end, because they are not thus prepared before death.

Thousands holding to milder forms of religion, among whom are not a few Universalists, as we have seen, have assumed the same position relative to the leading principle involved. "Neither death nor the resurrection," they say, "works any change in man's moral nature, or moral condition." "A change of worlds decides nothing as to the soul's essential moral condition." "Such a change will not make the slightest difference with us." "Passing from one room into another cannot change the character and the moral condition of a man, and *this* is all the change which is produced by a change of worlds." "We must take up the thread of life in the next world precisely where it was cut at the time of death in this." "All we ever are in this life or the next we must make ourselves." "All the salvation we can ever experience in this world or in Heaven, we shall receive only through our own efforts." *

These assertions are often made with much confidence as if they were self-evident truths and entirely in harmony with the declarations of the divine Word, when it is not possible they can contain one particle of truth, nor are they at all supported by the inspired Word. Consider for a moment what must be admitted, if all we have described as entertained by the parties mentioned is true.

---

* These are quotations from the writings of Universalist clergymen on the question involved.

1. If there is no change in man's moral nature at death or subsequently,—as our evangelical friends contend,—if those who enter the spiritual world sinners, will always remain in the same condition, then it is certain the whole human race will remain sinners through eternity, for *none die sinless.* There is no human being on earth, no matter how good and pure he is, or what his professions of righteousness, but *feels* the presence of indwelling sin and knows in his own soul, how very far from perfection he is. The Scriptures address all men as if they were weak, erring creatures, and affirm that "all come short of the glory of God." That "there is no "just man," even, "that liveth and sinneth not;"—while the beloved and saintly desciple John declared that "if we say we have no sin, we deceive ourselves and the truth is not in us."

Such is the nature and condition of *all* men *in this life,* as no one will attempt to deny. If, then, there is no change in the character or moral condition of any, only what is experienced in this life, then it follows of necessity, that all must possess the same *natures* and occupy precisely the same moral condition in which they die, forever. Heaven is a place of purity and holiness. The figures employed in the divine Word representing it, are strikingly beautiful. Its walls are said to be garnished with all manner of precious stones. Its foundations are of jasper and sapphire and emerald. Its gates are of pearls, every several gate a pearl, and its streets are of burnished gold as it were transparent glass, and so glorious is the purity of this beautiful place, that it is said to have no need of the sun, neither of the moon to shine in it, for the glory of God doth lighten it and the Lamb is the light thereof. And this is Heaven, the ultimate home of man! Yea, of all God's great family. How transcendentally pure, beautiful and glorious! And oh, how should our hearts glow with gratitude toward God for this unspeakable prospective blessing. But the same divine spirit that thus reveals Heaven as a place or condition of holiness, declares that "there shall in no wise enter into it anything *impure or that defileth, nor whatsoever worketh abomination or maketh a lie.*" Neither pride, nor envy, nor malice, nor revenge, nor any impure feeling, desire or thought can enter there. And yet all men,—regenerated though they may profess to have been,—are influenced more or less by all these ungodly emotions in this life. They sometimes permit themselves to cherish the most malicious feelings toward each other, to engage in the most abusive quarrels, to violate nearly every commandment of the decalogue and to be so filled with spite as to refuse to sit at the same communion table with their brethren, or in any possible way to fellowship them. Now, if there is no moral change in these men and others, by a change of worlds, then they will carry these feelings of malice with them into another life and retain them endlessly, hating and devouring each other forever. This is inevitable with all men, if they are to possess the same natures there as here, for the reason that all men are influenced more or less by them in this life. How then can ANY enter Heaven, or enjoy a heavenly condition? Every Christian who has ever lived has been excluded from Heaven from the beginning of the world, if only those enter that pure condition who are *fitted for it in this life, for none are fitted for it in this life.*

If, then, Heaven is the place or condition of sinless perfection it is represented to be, and none can enter there but those whose natures are in correspondence with the place, cannot the reader see that only one of two alternatives can possibly be true? First, either not one of the millions who have lived and died since the beginning of the world has entered there, or, second, in the process of the soul's resurrection from this body of sin and death into one of pure spirituality and glory, man is divested of the sinful elements of his being and retains only what in him is divine and celestial. And that the latter alternative is true beyond question, is abundantly manifest from the positive declarations of both Christ and the apostle who represent all as being raised "in incorruption," and "equal to the angels," as we shall see before we have done with the subject.

2. If we carry the same moral nature into the resurrection life we possess in this,—as not only the evangelical sects but many of the most liberal de-

nominations contend is true,—then all the lusts and passions, the sinful inclinations, the strong native appetites of our earthly organization must go with us and still inhere in our souls ; yea, they must enter into and constitute a part of our *constitutional nature* as really as they do in this world. Hence, it will also follow, that all the sins men are inclined to commit in this life they will desire to repeat in the world to come. If a man dies a drunkard or a libertine, or a thief, or a hypocrite, he will be raised into the immortal life a drunkard, a libertine, a thief, a hypocrite, with a nature, of course, that will incite to all these sins, and yet in that life his being must be purely and wholly spiritual. Can any person on careful reflection believe all this?

3. And if he *does* believe it, what assurance can he have that he can *ever* so subdue his nature of sin, even by prayer and constant effort, that he can rise into a condition of *perfect purity*, and thus enjoy a Heaven of divine, glorious and perfect rest and happiness? Surely, no man ever does, or ever *can* attain to such a condition of moral and spiritual purity and perfection in *this* life, and if he possesses the same nature in the future, the same passions, propensities, inclinations, lusts and appetites that enter into his nature here, what ground of belief has he that he shall ever utterly and eternally conquer them? Speculate as men may upon the subject, it is evident that if they still are a *part of him*, influencing him as they must, that not only a con-

dition of divine and angelic purity will be impossible with him, but, like good Christians in this world, he *may* be tempted and "drawn away of his own lusts and enticed" at any moment, yield to them, and so sin against God and his own soul in the other life as well as in this.

"It would please me," says an able and well-known defender of our faith, in a paper involving the subject of this writing, "to be informed why 'spiritual beings' cannot sin. Are they not moral beings?" We answer, if they possess the same *moral constitutions* they have in this life, they *will* sin—ALL WILL SIN, as we have shown above. The only security he or any other man can have against such a condition is that we shall *not* possess the same constitutional nature there as here. And this assurance is given in the plain and positive teachings of the Gospel which declare that sin is not perpetuated and immortalized, but vanquished and destroyed through the power and process of the resurrection. "The *last enemy* that shall be destroyed is death."

4. Then, again, if there is to be no radical change in us—if we are to possess the same minds with reference to all questions, and still be subjects of sin and the errors of this life, what advantage has the spiritual world over the present? Paul declared that "to depart and be with Christ is *far better*" than to remain in *the body*. Why *better* if we are still to be subjects of sin as when in the body?

Only imagine the Hottentots, Malays, Indians, Negroes and all the different tribes of the earth in the spiritual world in possession of the same moral natures—the same passions, dispositions, lusts and appetites they possess in this life! Instead of the charming, spiritual and blessed HOME the Christian now anticipates, what a pandemonium of error, passion, sin and wickedness that existence must be!

All this, we again affirm, we do not believe. It cannot be. A change of worlds is *not* simply passing out of one apartment into another; it is *not* merely like throwing off our garments as when we lie down to sleep, leaving us in possession of the same constitutional nature in the spiritual and immortal world which we possessed in this life. A change—great and wonderful—must take place in us by the power and process of the resurrection; and, if so, *what is the nature of that change?* To answer this question will be the object of our **next** chapter.

CHAPTER X.

What is the Nature of the Change Wrought by a Change of Worlds?

A Change of Worlds Necessitates a Change of Bodies.—Plain Teaching of the Apostle on this Subject.—Imperfection and Sinful Nature of our Physical Bodies, the Glory, Perfection and Wondrous Beauty of our Celestial Bodies.

"*DO you believe there will be any moral change in man on his passing from this world into the next ?*"

"*Shall we not be the same beings in the resurrection life that we are in this ?*"

In answer to the above questions we endeavored to show in the preceding chapter that man will not and *cannot* possess the same constitutional nature in the future life that he has in this ; that a change of worlds is not, as some affirm, simply the passing out of one apartment into another, without affecting our moral condition, or like throwing off our garments when we lie down to sleep, leaving us precisely the same beings, but that a change, great and wonderful, must take place in us and with us through the power and process of the resurrection. With us this fact is fully established, not only on the basis of reason but by the plain teachings of the New

Testament, and what all the outward facts in the case imperatively demand. If, then, such a change is produced by a change of worlds, *what is the nature of that change?*

We answer, first, that a change of worlds *necessitates a change of bodies.* In this life we inhabit physical bodies which were designed only for our earthly existence. Some of these bodies are very beautiful and attractive, and when in the bloom and vigor of young manhood or womanhood are often idolized. But as beautiful as they are, they "are of the earth, earthy;" will fade and wither and die, and hence were not designed for the perpetual and eternal habitation of the soul. When they cease to be animated with physical vitality, they turn to dust. The soul at death vacates them, and through the forces inherent in its nature, it is resurrected into a diviner condition, is clothed upon with a body purely spiritual and celestial, just as the butterfly, as we have before described, emerges from the gross material of the worm, and, clothed in a new and beautiful body, moves in a new and advanced sphere. Through a process, wonderful and inconceivable by man, this little insect has been transformed and elevated. By the change it has experienced, it is fitted for the new and exalted existence it occupies, and will never again return to its former condition of a worm.

This fact in natural history, which all *know to be a fact*, illustrates our idea of the change of bodies which takes place with human beings in a change of worlds. Only the change in man is much more radical. "It is sown a *natural* body, it is raised a *spiritual* body." The butterfly has no longer need of the material from which it has emerged; neither shall we have need of the material we shall leave in the grave. These physical limbs and organs, at the time of death, will have served man the purpose of God's design in their creation, and henceforward he will have no more use for them. They will return to dust, their native element, to be incorporated into new organisms, while *he* will pass into a more perfect condition of spiritual existence, and clothed upon with a new body, divine, celestial and spiritual, he will be fitted for the new, advanced and exalted sphere into which he will be raised.

As a Christian, possessing unbounded faith in the teachings of the Bible, we feel that this is not *speculation* but *reality*. If there is any one doctrine or sentiment plainly and positively taught in the divine Word it is the change which we describe. Look first at the luminous declarations of Paul on this subject as recorded in the 15th chapter of his first letter to the Corinthians. He asks: "How are the dead raised up and with *what body do they come?*" The inquiry is *not*, the reader will carefully notice, how those who die *leave this world;* or what was the nature of their faith and the peculiar condition of their minds at the moment of death. He does not ask whether their souls had been regenerated by the Holy Ghost, or whether they had lived in heathen or Christian lands. As interesting and important as are these questions so far as relates to our *present* existence and welfare, Paul has nothing to do with them when treating of the great doctrine of the resurrection and another life, as if upon the answers to *them* depends our immortal existence and the blessedness of the future world; but his question is, "How are the dead [those who die, or are dying] *raised up* and with WHAT BODY DO THEY COME?"

He answers,—and his answer is plain and to the point,—but singular enough, it affirms *precisely the contrary* of what has long been held to be true by many excellent Christians, who have said that the resurrection will take place thousands of years hence, perhaps, at the end of this material universe, or of Christ's mediatorial reign,—come when that time will,—and then the very bodies we inhabit at the time of death will be raised from their graves and again become the receptacles of our souls in which we shall stand before God for judgment, when, if it shall appear we were suitably prepared for heaven by regeneration, as we have before shown, we shall be received into glory and made happy and blessed forever; if not, we shall be cast away of God and consigned to realms of pain and suffering which shall never end.

The writer of these pages was once present at the

funeral of a wrinkled and decrepit old woman, whose age was four score and ten, and who for years had been dying with cancer in the neck. To our astonishment, the only consolation offered the mourners by the officiating clergyman,—a learned doctor of divinity,—was. that the identical body from which this old lady had escaped through death and the resurrection, would be raised at the judgment. We were also once present at the funeral of a cherub child, aged fifteen months. Its little body was white as alabaster and beautiful as the lilies with which it was decorated, when the minister informed the weeping parents, in substance, that the soul and body of their dear little babe would be buried in the grave where they would remain in God's keeping till the last great day at the end of time, when they would be resurrected from the grave and brought to God for judgment. But he told the parents they might take courage, as unquestionably the dear babe would be saved, for Christ loved little children, and if the parents would but "make their own calling and election sure" by turning to God in penitence, they would doubtless meet their loved one in heaven.

All this is cold comfort for the sorrowing mourner It lacks the beauty and vitality of Christian truth, and contains no blessing for the bereaved heart. More than this, it is contrary to the teachings of the divine Word, which no where intimates that the souls and bodies of those who die will be locked in the cold embrace of death till the end of this material world, at which time the veritable bodies we now inhabit, will be raised from the grave, re-animated with life and brought to the throne of God for judgment. Instead, no where in all the Bible is the assertion made or an intimation given that God will judge men in the resurrection life or that we go there for udgment, or that men will possess the same bodies there that they have here. On the contrary, the apostle declares in positive terms in answer to the question, "What shall be the character of our future bodies?" "Thou sowest not *that body that shall be.*" Employing a natural thing in illustration of his subject, he says:—"That which thou sowest is not *quickened, except it die.*" A grain of corn or of wheat is composed of the *body* or *lobes* and the *germ*. The body *dies*, and in a little while *decomposes*, when the *germ*, the *soul* of the wheat, is *quickened into newness of life*, and is clothed upon with a body, in likeness of the old, but created anew, by its vital, inherent forces, out of the elements of nature, so that this germ in its new existence will never again return and occupy the *old body* of the grain. So the apostle continues: "And that which thou sowest, thou sowest *not* THAT BODY WHICH SHALL BE * * *but God* GIVETH IT A BODY *as it hath pleased Him*, and to EVERY SEED HIS OWN BODY."

God gives us a body, when we enter this earthly existence, suited to our present needs. We shall be clothed upon with another body, when we shall be born into the higher, celestial life, which shall be suited to our new and exalted existence. The apostle proceeds:—"So also is the resurrection of the dead [those who die]. It is sown in corruption, it is raised in incorruption; it is sown in dishonor, it is raised in glory; it is sown a *natural* body, it is raised a *spiritual* body. * * . Howbeit that was not first which was spiritual, but that which is natural; *afterward* that which is spiritual. * * As is the earthy, such are they also that are earthy; and as is the heavenly, such are they also that are heavenly; and as *we have borne the image of the earthy we shall also bear the image of the heavenly.*" The *process*, he says, is similar, but the change more *radical* than that which takes place in the germination and growth of the wheat.

And this is said, not of the righteous, of saints, or of any *elected* and *special* class only, but of *all who die*, or of *all human beings*, for the bodies of all are mortal. This world is not our abiding place. The bodies we inhabit in this existence contain the seeds of death and decay. God in His wisdom and goodness so designed. But thanks to the grace of that great and good Being, who is our Father, the death and dissolution of our bodies do not destroy *us*. Indeed, this change, as we have before shown, is indispensable that we may enter a more exalted condition. The *germ* of the corn cannot be *quickened* EXCEPT its *body* dies.

How plain and positive this instruction, and how comforting the truth which it develops in describing the change wrought by the power and process of the resurrection. When what we call death takes place with us, these mortal bodies fall to decay, when we shall be clothed upon with celestial, and far more beautiful and glorious structures. "The glory of the celestial is one, and the glory of the terrestial is another." *

"Here," says an eminent writer on the New Testament,† "the glory, the excellence, beauty and perfection of our future spiritual body is referred to. Even the present *frail, human body* possesses an indescribable degree of contrivance, art, economy, order, beauty and excellence; but the *celestial* body, that in which Christ now appears and according to which ours shall be, ‡ will exceed the excellence of this beyond comparison. A *glory* or *splendor* will belong to that which does not belong to this; *here* there is a glory of excellence; *there* there will be a glory of light and effulgence; for the bodies of the glorified spirits shall shine like the sun in the kingdom of their Father."

Here, then, is established the fact of our assertion at starting; that a change of worlds necessitates a *change of bodies*. Paul says "there *is* a natural body and there *is* a spiritual body." We will not attempt in these pages to go into the philos-

---
* 1 Cor. 15:40.
† Dr. Adam Clark, the learned Methodist Commentator.
‡ Phil. 3:21.

ophy of the formation or development of the new spiritual body—how it is organized or from what substance! *That* is not our present object. We are not *now* writing to convince skeptics of the fact of a spiritual existence. We deem our arguments in former chapters on this subject conclusive; but we would convince Christians of the *nature* and *condition* of that existence. It is enough for our present purpose to know what the New Testament asserts relative to the change of which we speak. In this world we inhabit sinful bodies;—bodies of lusts, appetites, passions. In the future, from the foregoing instruction, how wonderfully changed will be our condition in this respect. And, as if to render the theme still more plain and luminous, Paul says again,* as we have before quoted in illustration of another point:—

"For we *know* that if our earthly house of this tabernacle were dissolved, we have a building of God, an house not made with hands, eternal in the heavens." Here the assurance is that we shall inhabit in the future existence, not the old building renovated, but a new *building of God—spiritual, beautiful and eternal* in its nature. "For in this," [*earthly* tabernacle] saith the apostle, "we groan, earnestly desiring to be clothed upon with our *house which is from Heaven* * * that mortality might be swallowed up of life."

How can language be framed to teach more posi-

---
* 2 Cor. 5:1.

tively not only a change of bodies in the resurrection, but to afford assurance of the superior purity, beauty and celestial splendor of the future body? Continues the apostle, "For in *this* [body] we groan, being burdened" with the pains, sins, weariness and perplexities of our mortal existence; but when clothed with our new celestial body, we shall be delivered from this "bondage of corruption into the glorious liberty of the children of God," when all that is mortal in our being shall be "swallowed up of life." Then there "shall be no more death [spiritual or literal], neither sorrow nor crying, neither shall there be any more pain, for the former things are passed away."*

The apostle closes what he has to say on this sublime subject with the words: "We are always confident, and willing *rather to be absent from the body* [earthly body] *and present with the Lord.*" By which all men are assured of these three things: First, that the soul will not sleep in the grave to the end of time and then be resuscitated with the body; nor Second, shall it enter a conscious condition of sinfulness and wretchedness, a kind of purgatory, where by prayer and spiritual effort we shall prepare ourselves for Christ's presence; but Third, when the body dies, when "our earthly house of this tabernacle is dissolved," we shall *then* take possession of our new, beatific, celestial, spiritual building, "that house not made with hands,

---
* Rev. 21:4.

eternal in the heavens," and *"be present with the Lord."*

Does all this look as if man is precisely the same being in the immortal life he is in this? But this subject will be considered more at length in our next chapter.

>   Far from these scenes of night
>   Unbounded glories rise,
>   And realms of infinite delight,
>   Unknown to mortal eyes.
>   No cloud these regions know,
>   Forever bright and fair;
>   For sin, the source of mortal woe,
>   Can never enter there.
>
>   There night is never known,
>   Nor sun's faint, s'ckly ray;
>   But glory from th' eternal throne
>   Spreads everlasting day.
>   Oh, may this prospect fire
>   Our hearts with ardent love!
>   And lively faith and strong desire
>   Bear every thought above.

CHAPTER XI.

A Change of Bodies not the only Change Man Experiences by a Change of Worlds.

Difference between the Terrestrial and Celestial Body.—The Purity and Glory of the Latter.—Can this Radical Change take place with Man and not affect him as a Moral Being?—Can a sinful Soul occupy a sinless Body?

"WILL *there be no moral change in man on his passing from this world into the next?*"

"*Shall we be the same beings in the Resurrection life we are in this?*"

By the facts presented in the last preceding chapter, from the positive testimony of an inspired apostle, we have seen something of the wonderful change produced in the outward condition of man by a change of worlds, and the almost inconceivable dissimilarity between his *terrestrial* and his *celestial* body. In this life, we "bear the image of the earthy;" in the future, we shall bear "the image of the heavenly." Here our bodies are frail, imperfect, sinful; there, they shall be powerful, spiritual, holy, glorious. Here they are subjects of disease and death; there we shall inhabit bodies subject to no such infirmities, for they will be immortal, celestial, eternal. Here very many are shockingly deformed physically, or old, withered, wrinkled and crippled when they die; there they will be clothed upon with eternal youth and celestial beauty. Here our bodies are full of corruption, possessing fleshly lusts, appetites, propensities and passions, but there, liberated from these, our bodies will be fashioned like Christ's glorious body—as seen in the transfiguration on the mount in the spiritual presence of Moses and Elias, when "his face did shine as the sun, and his raiment became shining, and exceeding white as snow."

This is the *nature* of the *bodies* we shall inhabit in the resurrection life, or Paul was deceived and the New Testament is full of error and a lie, for no doctrine of the Gospel is more plainly and positively taught in the sacred Word than this.

Now we have said in these pages that the *body* is not *the man,*—by which we mean the thinking, reasoning, divine principle which constitutes him God's child,—but only the house he lives in; but, still, all know that there is a very close and intimate relation and connection between the two, so that man is constantly influenced by the passions and lusts of the flesh in this life. And is it not reasonable to suppose that he will also be equally influenced by his surroundings in the future? And, if so, can it be possible the marvelous, radical change we have described can take place with him, and he still remain precisely the same moral being, in all particulars, he was while a dweller in the flesh? This is what men tell us, but can it be possible, considering the two natures,—*terrestrial* and *celestial*,—man bears in his outward being in this world and the next? See how positive the language of the apostle :—"It [the man] is sown in corruption, but is raised [not *shall* be at the end of time, but *is*] in incorruption; it is sown in dishonor, it is raised in glory; it is sown in weakness, it is raised in power; it is sown a natural body, it is raised a spiritual body."

The future body, then, unlike the nature of man's *present* body, is to be one of *incorruption, glory, power,* and purely *spiritual*. And this is to be the outward *nature* and *condition* of *all* God's great family in the future life, for the declaration is that all who "bear the image of the earthy, shall also bear the image of the heavenly." And we ask again, can the wonderful change thus described be limited to our bodies? Will it not necessarily affect *us?* Are the *bodies* of men to be made thus wonderfully powerful, spiritual, glorious and celestial in the future world, while their *souls* are to remain in the same condition of weakness and dishonor, littleness, wretchedness and corruption they are in while dwellers in the flesh? Will there be no change in the nature of the soul's affections? In the objects of its loves, its ability to comprehend, or the nature and strength of its aspirations? Will the casket be thus wonderfully prepared, shining and glowing with divine purity and beauty, all through and through, only to receive and retain the same sinful, dwarfed, selfish soul that inhabited its impure body on earth?

This is what men say. *All* evangelical sects say it so far as we know ; and all others who contend that man himself is not changed at all morally by a change of worlds, unreasonable, illogical and contrary to philosophy and the nature of things as it is, are forced to this interpretation. Here is the great change, certainly and positively taught by the apostle, and if they admit that it affects *the souls* of men for the better, it affects their theory of salvation, and their whole system totters to its fall, and so they affirm that the change described by the apostle refers only to our bodies. We have presented, in a previous chapter, the animated description of the resurrection body, as given by a leading commentator. * In the most glowing language, he depicts its purity, beauty, brightness, glory and effulgence, and yet he renders the whole ridiculous by saying, further along, that these beatific, celestial bodies are to be occupied by dwarfed and sinful souls and the whole consigned to the regions of the damned, where they will be made to suffer as long as the throne of God should endure !

Can we conceive of anything more unreasonable than this hypothesis, or revolting to the soul of one whose faith in God and hope of immortality are based on the sweet and hopeful instructions of Christ and his apostles? In direct contrast with the

---

* Dr. Adam Clark.

above we find another eminent writer * on the New Testament, who has the entire confidence of his denomination, in commenting on the same Scripture, making use of it in proof of his faith in the purification and salvation of all men. He says:—"If this language describes the resurrection body, only, it needs nothing more to show that the resurrection state is one of universal holiness and happiness; for it would be difficult to show how a soul, dwelling in an incorruptible, glorious, spiritual body, could be unholy and miserable. No soul, in such a heavenly habitation as is here portrayed by Paul, could possibly be in a moral condition, or in a state of suffering, represented by the word 'hell.'"

These are precisely our views. We can not conceive it possible that a soul of sin,—a drunken or lying or thievish or adulterous or murderous soul,— or a soul in any sense corrupt, could dwell in such a body. Nor can we conceive it possible that such a body, purely spiritual and divine, could, in any way, tempt or incite the soul to sin as do our bodies of lust and psasion in this life. The same apostle who affords us instruction so full and hopeful relative to the facts and nature of the resurrection and the purity and glory of our celestial bodies, is careful to impress us with the influence which the lusts, appetites and passions of our physical nature have over the soul, so long as we are connected with our present bodies, by placing before us what he de-

† Rev. T. B. Thayer in his "Theology of Universalism," page 241.

nominates the *"works of the flesh,"* in the following dark catalogue. He says * "Now the works of the flesh are manifest, which are these: adultery, fornication, uncleanness, lasciviousness, idolatry, hatred, variance, emulations, wrath, strife, seditions, heresies, envyings, murders, drunkenness, revelings and such like." Here is a catalogue which embraces, under either one or the other terms employed, every sin that can be named, and the apostle calls them the "works of the flesh," by which he means that they are committed through the influences of incitement and temptation, either directly or indirectly, on the soul. The reader will please notice that though the apostle here denominates sin "the works of the flesh," he does not make the physical body the *responsible sinner ;* and he will please bear in mind also that *we* do not. It is enough for *us*, as a Christian, to follow Christ and his apostles. We do not believe any man can improve on their truth or their philosophy. Paul's *body* was not Paul. It was the house he occupied while connected with *material* things. That body died and mouldered back to dust, its native element, while Paul himself, through the resurrection, was clothed upon with a body purely spiritual, of divine glory and sinless perfection, as we have described.

When he was a dweller in his physical body, so interwoven was his spiritual being with it—so under its *influence* and *control* that, yielding to those in-

---
* Gal. 5:19.

fluences, it sometimes occasioned him to sin; and yet *it* was never *responsible* for any act he committed, any more than the clothes he wore were responsible. He says:—"I find then a law, that, when I would do good, evil is present with me. For I delight in the law of God after the inward man; but I see another law in my members, warring against the law of my mind, and bringing me into captivity to the law of sin which is in my members." Here he keeps up the distinction between *himself* and his *body*. "The law of sin" was "in his members," and yet *he* was the responsible head, and these "members" all belonged to him and were under his control. If he yielded to the lusts and temptations of his physical nature, which were clamoring to lead him astray, by this act, *he* became a sinner, and before God *he*—not his *body*—must answer for the offense committed.

Now what we desire specially to enforce is the simple idea that in all this the reader can behold the *nature* and *strength* of the influence of our present bodies, over our souls. And hence, it must be that when liberated utterly from the shackles of these appetites and passions, and lifted up out of them, being clothed upon with pure, spiritual and celestial vestments, divine and glorious, and become of heaven, heavenly, such will be the superior nature of our surroundings and their holy influence when compared with our condition in this life, that *we ourselves*—our *souls*—must be renovated, elevated in thought, and rendered more pure in our desires and conceptions. To us it seems impossible that such a change can take place in the "outer man" and in all his outward surroundings, without producing a corresponding change in the "inner man ;"—we mean in *him*, as a child of God, a moral and spiritual being.

We *know* he can no longer be a subject of physical appetite, lust or passions; no longer be guilty of drunkenness, or adultery, or of any of the many sins enumerated by the apostle as the works of the flesh, for the reason that he will no longer possess the same constitutional nature he has in this life; and though the soul will have its delights, and enjoy them in a degree a thousand fold greater than in this world. it will no longer have pleasure in sinful indulgences, but delight only in celestial enjoyments.

From all this it will be seen that a change of worlds *must* "decide *something* essential as to man's moral condition ;"—that, being born out of the earthly into the heavenly *does* "make a difference with him ;"—that his salvation from sin is *not* entirely through his own efforts ;—that he *is* something "in the future life besides what he makes himself," or he would be indeed a poor subject for Heaven ;— that, though he fully retains his identity as God's child, he is not and cannot be "precisely the same being in the resurrection life he is here," for he is no longer a sinner in that life, while the best of men are sinners in this life,—and hence he does *not* and *cannot* "take up the thread of his existence in the other world precisely where it was cut at the time of death in this world," and all the assertions to the contrary, so often made, are simply denials of the plain and positive teachings of the divine Word and should have no influence with the soul of the Christian. He should look only to Christ and confide in his blessed word. Nothing can be more beautiful or comforting than his truth.

"He comes the broken heart to bind,
The bleeding soul to cure."

But "broken hearts and bleeding souls" can be bound and cured only with the balm of the Gospel as it emanated from its divine author:—

"He came to earth from a land of love,
To dry our tearful eyes,
To tell us of our home above,
Beyond the mortal skies.

"He came with power to conquer death,
To break the chains of fear,
To ope the gates of spirit life,
And show its shining mere.

"To soothe our spirits bowed with pain,
To answer doubts that sting,
And to the hearts where sorrows reign
A balm of Gilead bring.

"He came, he came from realms of light,
To lead us to the shore
Where angels dwell in sweet delight
Forever, evermore."

CHAPTER XII.

Elevating and Renovating Power of the Resurrection.

The Scriptural Usage of the Word Anastasis, translated Resurrection.—It is sometimes applied to Man's Moral and Spiritual Up-rising.—Its meaning as Employed by the Apostle in describing Man's Birth into the Other Life.—Out of the Mortal into the Immortal.—Out of the Earthly into the Heavenly.—The Glory of the Future Life when compared with this.

WE come now to say that the objector may take exceptions to our views concerning the moral and spiritual change effected in man through the resurrection, on the grounds that the Gospel usage of the term *anastasis*, or resurrection, which is said to be applied *only* to the resuscitation of something that had literally died, like a human corpse, will permit no such application of the term as we have made of it. We are aware that this is the general impression relative to the usage of this word, but it is a great mistake. The word *anastasis*, generally translated resurrection, though often employed by the sacred writers to denote the resuscitation of dead bodies, does not necessarily imply that those to whom it refers should be dead. It is often applied to those who are living and signifies a *quickening*, a *raising up*, an *exaltation* or *elevation*.

Hence, arising from a seat, awaking out of sleep, elevated in office, or position, or circumstances, is properly termed *anastasis*. In this sense it is employed by Simeon concerning Christ, when he said: "Behold this child is set for the fall and rising [*anastasis*] again of many in Israel;" which had reference only to the temporal, moral and spiritual condition of the Jews, as a consequence of Christ's mission and teachings. The word is used in a similar sense in many other places, as we might show were it necessary, where it is applied to living persons and has reference to their moral or spiritual elevation. As employed in the New Testament by Paul and Christ, concerning the passing of human beings out of this mortal life into the immortal, it implies, as we have seen, the quickening, exaltation and renovation of the *man*—of the spiritual of his nature, rather than the grosser elements of his being.

Hence, when Paul asks:—"How are the dead [those who are passing out of this life] raised up?" he means to include *the man*, rather than his literal body; and when he proceeds to discuss the present and future condition of human beings, and unfolds the great doctrine of our birth out of this earthly life into the heavenly and divine, he embraces something beside the gross material of his *earthly* nature. This, wonderful as is its contrivance, and as necessary as it is as the habitation of man while connected with his earthy being, is not *the man*. It has no power of thought,—no affectional impulses, no will, no conscience, no divine aspirations, and yet, see how the apostle makes the future body sparkle and glow with celestial purity and glory through the resurrection power, in the other life. And if all this is certain of the body,—the casket, —what shall we not hope for the soul, the jewel, —the man himself included as is his *entire nature*, as God's child, in the all-quickening, elevating and renovating power of the resurrection, as described in the language already quoted:—"It is sown in corruption," "dishonor," "weakness;" but raised in "*incorruption,*" "*glory,*" "*power!*"

And all this is implied in the term *anastasis* as applied by Paul to the up-rising or resurrection of man, into a future and higher life. All the powers of his soul are improved by this transition; all his aspirations corrected and intensified, and his entire being exalted and brought more into harmony with the pure and divine. Yea, in the language of Rev. Dr. Thayer, in the work just now referred to,—"The resurrection is not simply being lifted out of the mortal into the immortal,—out of the earthly into the heavenly; but out of the imperfect into the perfect,—out of the weakness and frivolity and sinfulness of our present state, into the strength and holiness and spiritual completeness of the future state."

Comforting and hopeful as is this sublime doctrine, we believe it is fully sustained by the language of the apostle in the Scripture under consideration, not with reference to a select class of the human family only, but concerning every sentient creature born into this world. If the reader still doubts the truth of what we affirm on the grounds that the change described by Paul, through the *anastasis* or resurrection power, is simply a *bodily* change and has nothing to do with the man as a moral and spiritual being, we would call his attention to a more careful and particular consideration of what the apostle affirms, and what must be admitted on the supposition that a bodily change is alone referred to; and, we do this, not merely to multiply words on the subject, but to convince him of the truth of what the divine Word really teaches on this subject, as we regard it one of great moment. The apostle positively declares, in this connection, not only that all men shall be raised in a condition of "incorruption" and "glory," etc., but also that in the resurrection life they shall all bear "the image of the heavenly."

Now the hypothesis that in all this the apostle has no reference to the resurrection of man's moral or spiritual being, but only to his bodily nature, cannot possibly be correct, for the following reasons:

1. Because, if it has no reference to man's moral or spiritual nature, then in the resurrection he will be in the same condition precisely as a moral being that he is in this world; but how can a man whose moral nature is corrupt, wicked, devilish, be said, in any proper sense, to be "glorious"—or to

"bear the image of the heavenly?" A *heavenly* image cannot possibly belong to a soul of *wickedness*.

2. Because if the above instruction has reference only to men's *bodies*, then it affords us no assurance that man himself will be raised at all, but only his body. This is to be restored to life and made immortal, incorruptible, glorious, heavenly, while *he* is unnoticed, repudiated.

3. Because it is evident that the apostle meant by the phrases he employed, to include the whole man in the raising as well as in the sowing. He says. "It is sown in corruption, it is raised in incorruption," etc. No distinct definition is here given of what is implied in the word "*it*." But this we know, that the same phrase is employed in the raising as in the sowing, which shows that whatever was included in the one was also included in the other; so that when the apostle said, "*it* is raised in incorruption,' he meant more than the *animal body*. Indeed, the animal body, the grosser elements of it—the bones, the flesh, the hair, the teeth, etc., etc., are never resuscitated, and yet man will possess a "body" in the future existence. "*It* is sown a natural body; *it* is raised a *spiritual* body." Transformation takes place, as we have seen, when the unsightly worm, by a process of nature, is changed into a gorgeous butterfly. The new body is not the same with the old body, though it bears a certain relation to it. It is now so surpassingly

beautiful and moves in a sphere so different, and with powers and capacities so enlarged from those of its former condition of a loathsome worm, crawling in the dust, that no human penetration is sufficient to discover in it *the same* creature. Nor is it the same precisely in a strict sense. The one has been metamorphosed into the other. The one is from, or out of the other.

"It,"—referring to the whole insect,—was sown a worm, with the characteristics and instincts of a butterfly. Instead of crawling in filth, it now flits from flower to flower,—subsists on nectar and soars aloft in the light and glory of heaven,—and so resplendent in beauty is it, that it attracts and delights all who comprehend the wonderful change wrought.

So of man, as represented by the apostle in the Scripture under consideration. Having declared that all who die shall be made alive IN CHRIST—and hence become new creatures spiritually and morally —he goes on to describe the condition in which they shall exist in their new state in the resurrection. "So, also is the resurrection of the dead. It is sown in corruption, it is raised in incorruption." The reader will see, we repeat, that the verbs *sown* and *raised* have no expressed nominatives. *What* is sown and *what* is raised, is not specially defined. Stanley says the meaning of the original is best rendered by the phrase "there is a sowing"—"there is a raising." "Throughout this parallel, the image of the verb," he says, "is taken from the seed."

"It," meaning the seed, is sown. This is our view, and hence, something more is meant by the word "it," we repeat, than is included in the body, for when we sow a kernel of corn or wheat, we not only deposit the *outside* lobes of the kernel, but the *internal* germ of life. We sow, indeed, all there is of the seed. So when the apostle says, "*It* is sown in corruption, *it* is raised in glory," etc., he refers to all there is included in the being of man— what we call *his* death and *his* resurrection; the nature and character of his existence here, and the nature and character of his existence in the other life. And yet, though we speak of the death of *man* when his *body* dies, really or literally, *he* no more dies, than does the caterpillar in being metamorphosed into a butterfly.

He is "sown" a man, with the nature and characteristics of a man,—subject to corruption in body and thought,—to dishonor and weakness because of the lusts and passions of the flesh,—but is raised with a nature, character and instincts more angelic. In the future he will be incorruptible, glorious and powerful, because his nature will be purely spiritual. He did bear the image of the earthy; he now bears the image of the heavenly, and hence can be no longer a subject of the corrupting influences of this life. Indeed, Christ declares that in that life they are *as the angels*, being the children of the resurrection. And Paul, in summing up the whole, in the chapter containing the above, pronounces the

same glorious truth in the following language:—
"*When* this corruptible shall have put on incorruption and this mortal shall have put on an immortality, *then* shall be brought to pass the saying that is written, 'death is swallowed up in victory;'" which is equivalent to the declaration of the 26th verse that in the resurrection "Death, the LAST ENEMY, shall be destroyed."* If death is man's *last* enemy, how can sin and corruption and sorrow and wretchedness still continue? And this condition of spirituality, incorruptibility and glory comes from the sowing and the raising or the *anastasis*—resurrection—described by the apostle in the language we have had under consideration. And thus it will be seen that we have employed this term [*anastasis*] correctly in these pages, and that Paul applied the words "incorruption," "power," "glorious," etc., to the *spiritual* and *moral* of man's nature,—or to the man himself,—rather than to the *material* of his nature, and meant by it that in the future life,— a life of entire spirituality,—man would no longer possess a sinful nature and hence no longer be a

---

* These ideas, however they may strike some minds who have not fully investigated the subject, as being unfounded in the Scriptures, are sustained by some of the greatest and best men. For instance, Rev. Dr. Chalmers says:—"Before death sin is only repressed,—after the resurrection sin will be exterminated. Here the believer has to maintain the combat, with a tendency to evil still lodging in his heart, and working a perverse movement among his inclinations; but after his warfare in this world is accomplished, he will no longer be so thwarted. The great constitutional plague of his nature will no longer trouble him, and there will be a charm of genial affinity between the purity of his heart and the purity of the element he breathes in."—*Chalmers' Sermon on 2 Peter,* 3:13.

subject of the weakness and corrupting influence of sin, but would be elevated, purified and blest.

In our next chapter we shall strengthen what we have said, by the consideration of other facts intimately related to the subject in question.

"There is a land mine eye hath seen,
In visions of enraptured thought,
So bright that all which spreads between
Is with its radiant glory fraught :—

"A land upon whose blissful shore
There rests no shadow, falls no stain;
There those who meet shall part no more,
And those long parted meet again.
* * * * *

"There sweeps no desolating wind
Across that calm, serene abode;
The wanderer there a home will find,
Within the paradise of God."

CHAPTER XIII.

Excellence and Perfection of our Future Bodies.

The Soul.—Sin, how does it Originate?—The Spiritual Body not only Beautiful but Perfect.—Hence, no such mistakes as Sin are made in the Future.—The Spiritual Brain.—Wonderful Powers of the Soul when in a Mesmeric Trance.—What may not be its possibilities in the Resurrection Life when relieved of the Clogs of the Flesh?—The Cape Ann Clairvoyant Boy.—The Somnambulist and of what he is capable.

THE reader who has followed us thus far, begins to perceive by this time, something of the grandeur and glory of this great theme,—a theme which relates so intimately to God and Heaven and glory. We are sometimes told that all this is too good to be true! But there is nothing too good or beautiful to proceed from a God of infinite perfection. The truth is, the great mistake of the vast body of professed Christians is, that they doubt God, have too low an estimate of His goodness, and of the future beauties and glories of our home in Heaven. They talk of the other world as if it were similar to this,—filled with the same imperfections and controlled by the same influences, when the Bible everywhere describes it as one greatly exalted, as of pure spirituality, and as being resplendent with glory. So far in advance is it, compared with the present life, that Paul declares it impossible for the human soul in this existence, with its limited capacity, to entertain anything like a correct conception of its wonders, its delights, its glories.* The tendency of everything that will go to make up our nature in the future life, will be to protect us from error and wrong and defilement. We have spoken of the superior beauty and purity of our future bodies; we will now add that these spiritual structures for the future habitation of the soul, will be not only pure and beautiful, but *perfect in their organization*, as must be all things in the heavenly life, and hence the spiritual organs, so to speak, through which the soul will act, will be such that the ignorance and mistakes of our present existence will not be possible in the future, which is another powerful reason for the belief that sin will not be possible in that existence. For sin is the result not only of the impure desires and passions of our physical nature, but of almost utter ignorance of what is for our best good.

Of what constitutes the essence or substance of the soul, no man has any absolute knowedge. But every man is conscious that he *has* a soul, by which we mean a thinking, reasoning principle, and however strongly he may disbelieve in the existence of *disembodied* spirits, it needs no argument, as we have before stated, to convince him of the existence of *his own* spirit. There is no substance in thought, but the thing that thinks *must be constituted of something*.

---
* 1 Cor. 2:9.

When God created man of the dust of the earth, he breathed into his nostrils the breath of life, and *man became a living soul.* This demonstrates the fact of which we have before spoken in these pages, that *the body* is not *the man;*—but his soul is the man. Man became a *living soul.* Now, we repeat, no man has knowledge of what constitutes the *essence* or *substance* of this "living soul," or the man, any more than he has knowledge of what constitutes the essence or substance of God.

The divine Word declares that "God is a Spirit." We believe that the soul of man is purely spiritual. We do not believe that it possesses the elements of the body, nor do we believe that as connected with the physical brain, or in its disembodied state a subject of the resurrection,—it is ever polluted in the elements and substance of its being, by sin. All know how various sins taint and pollute and corrupt man's physical nature, resulting, in some instances, in the absolute and literal death of the body. But no such taint or pollution ever touches literally the spiritual essence or substance of the soul. We do not believe that the element or essence which constitutes a ray of sunlight, or the electrical agent, can be tainted or polluted, much less the material of the soul. In a certain sense, it is of heaven, heavenly. Hence, we do not believe that it possesses any element that *inherently incites to sin.* Do not let us be misunderstood here. We believe that the soul, the thinking, reasoning, immortal principle, that constitutes the man—is the responsible head or agent in all moral acts, and yet we do not believe that inherently the essence or substance of the soul possesses any element in its nature that would move or impel him to sin.* But, nevertheless, it is a *subject of temptation.* It is swayed by the appetites and passions of the fleshly nature in whose organization it is interwoven. If there were no temptation there would be no sin. If there were nothing to attract us in the wrong direction we should never be found in the way of wrong. But we are not only tempted, but we are ignorant and weak, we yield and fall, and this is the way in which the apostle explains the *cause* and the *process* of sin. He says: "Every man is tempted, when he is drawn away of his own lust and enticed. Then when lust hath conceived, *it bringeth forth sin."* If we could always prevent the conception of the "lusts of the flesh;— in other words, if like Christ, we were always wise enough, and strong enough, to resist all temptation, then, like him, we should be without sin.

Now we believe that in the future life—a life of pure spirituality, we shall not only be lifted up out of this body of sin, that by its appetites tempts and incites to evil, but we shall be clothed upon with a spiritual body, as we have before seen, which will be equally free from any inherent element of sin

---

* We would regard it a favor if the reader will consider carefully what we say in this connection, and not represent us as advocating the idea that the body not only sins but is responsible for sin. We advocate no such impossibility.

with the soul itself, and, therefore the soul will never more be in a condition of possibility to temptation. And, besides, as we say at the beginning of this chapter, such will be the perfection of the future spiritual structure, for the habitation of the soul, and hence perfection of the celestial machinery, so to speak, through which the soul will act, that the ignorance and mistakes consequent on our present imperfect structure can never be known in the future life.

Probably the substance and essence of the soul itself is very similar in all persons. The apparent difference in the intellects of men is mainly in consequence of a real difference in the brains through which they develop themselves. The more perfect the brain, the more perfect *appears* to be the mind, but really the *substance* of the soul is as perfect in one as another. The idiot is not an idiot because he has no intellect, or because it is not as perfect in the essence and substance of its being as yours or ours, but because of the malformation of the brain. He has no instrumentalities through which he can develop; no tools with which to work. The soul exists there perfect, but the brain is chaotic, and hence the darkness of the soul.

But in the resurrection this shall not be. This benighted soul, thanks to God, shall not remain in this unfortunate condition forever. This would be its doom, inevitably, if our life in the flesh were endless. Let the tender-souled mother and affectionate father who have so pitied their poor, idiotic child, and have mourned and wept over him, and tended and protected him with care and assiduity so great;—who have felt a tenderness for this child that they have never experienced toward the more favored children of their affection, take courage and rejoice, for, through death and the resurrection, the dear one shall be released from his present imperfect physical structure, and be made a partaker of the blessedness that is the result of celestial perfection.

All his life long here, this child has learned comparatively nothing, he has enjoyed nothing, and made no progress. In the future, he shall be clothed upon with as perfect and glorious a vesture as the most advanced soul. His spiritual brain—if we can be allowed this accommodate expression—shall be marred with no imperfection in its essence or structure, as in this life. Hence, the idiot here, cannot be an idiot there, but through the transforming power of the resurrection he shall be put in possession of instrumentalities for spiritual growth and advancement in love, in knowledge, and in all that shall go to make the sum of happiness, equal to the more favored in this life. And this advancement out of the imperfect brain into the divine and perfect, shall be experienced *by all of every degree of mental or spiritual development ;* and hence the future to all shall be one far in advance of the present, as to the purity and perfection of our organized being and our increased means of growth in all that is spiritual, beatific and divine. Hence, all have reason to be thrilled with joy and gratitude to God, in view of the unspeakable blessing the hope of another life as revealed in the Gospel, affords the soul. How priceless is the worth of this great boon! In addition to all this, it is our belief that in that exalted condition, the soul will obtain knowledge by processes different from those by which it is obtained in this life. Now, we stumble in darkness; then, floods of light shall surround us. We shall live and move in our future home, in the noonday sunshine of the beauties and glory of the immortal existence, and knowledge will flash through the soul intuitively. Why should not this be true, while even here, when connected with the gross element of the physical brain, the mind can be thrown into that condition in which it is brought to receive truthful impressions and *absolutely* to *know* relative to a thousand wonderful things in nature without study or any apparent mental effort, as when in what we regard a normal condition.

When in a mesmeric trance, a girl twelve years of age, and psychologically under our control, was able without failure to describe the exact character of strangers, their maladies, how long they had been sick, the nature of the medicines they had employed, where they had resided, etc. How was this knowledge obtained? We answer, either intuitively or by a method of the soul we do not now comprehend.

How can the hound trace the track of the hare? We have had the mesmeric subject mentally follow back our tracks, and tell us every place we had visited through the day, and what had been the nature of our occupation, what we had said and done. In this condition they can read the thoughts of other minds.

Twenty years ago, a little boy was living on Cape Ann, who had the power of discovering vessels thirty miles distant at sea, and describing their cargoes. When the most powerful glass would reveal nothing of their approximation, he would not only describe the vessel and cargo but the number of men on board. He possessed the ability to throw himself into a kind of magnetic or clairvoyant state, and saw, he said, by means of a bright, luminous appearance which opened before him in whatever direction he turned his attention. This is the declaration and explanation of all clairvoyants. Science reveals the existence of a luminiferous ether which is supposed to be diffused through every part of the material universe. It is described as an exceedingly subtile and active fluid, and seems to be the agent by which light and electricity are transmitted in undulations in every direction, with the most inconceivable velocity. But it is not cognizable by any of the senses when the soul is in its normal condition. When, however, the soul is brought upon a higher plane through the process or phenomena of mesmerism, the agent of which we speak seems to be an all pervading element, and is to the soul what electricity is to the battery. So that when in this abnormal condition, even while connected with the flesh, what wonderful powers of knowledge the soul possesses. And is it not reasonable to suppose that in the resurrection with its increased instrumentalities, it shall possess *still greater* ability?

No one doubts the common form of somnabulism called sleep-walking. "A person in this state makes no use of his natural vision. His eyes are like those of a corpse. You may hold a light so near to them as to singe the eyelashes, and he will neither perceive you nor the light; and yet he walks in the most dangerous places in the darkest night unharmed." These are facts which no one doubts. Nor is this all. When in this condition, the soul not unfrequently is in possession of knowledge and grasps principles concerning which it is utterly ignorant in a wakeful state. Repeated instances are recorded of persons arising from their beds and writing poems, orations and the like, containing expression of thoughts and discussing principles far beyond their capacity in the normal state. And besides this, they have sometimes worked out, when in this condition, the most difficult problems in mathamatics;—problems they could not possibly comprehend when awake. We repeat, if all this is true of the soul while connected with its imperfect brain of flesh, who will say that even greater things shallnot be true of it when in a glorified state, in possession of its perfect, spiritual, celestial brain?

Taking St. Paul's declarations concerning the condition of the whole being of man in the resurrection, it is impossible for us to conceive that man will not, by the resurrection, be put in possession of the means of learning and knowing, far in advance of any such gift in his position in this life. All truth is spiritual. In the future, we must have it in a greater degree than we experience on earth. The clogs of the flesh must be removed. The soul will be clothed upon with its divine and radiant garment, and drinking in knowledge of God, of Heaven, of the nature and mysteries of the universe, it shall progress forever and ever in study, in knowledge and discovery in the great and sublime principles that underlie the government of God in the universe.

And so death is really no curse to man but a blessing, because it is the step indispensable to the resurrection. The "immortal Young" has truthfully expressed the Christian idea, when he says:—

"*Death* is the crown of *life*;
Were death denied, poor man would live in vain;
Were death denied, to live would not be life;
Were death denied, e'en fools would wish to die.
Death wounds to cure; we fall, we rise, we reign!
Spring from our fetters, foster in the skies.
This king of terrors is the prince of peace.
When shall I die to vanity, pain, death?
When shall I die, that I may live forever?"

In our next chapter we shall show how positively all this is sustained by the teaching of the Gospel, —especially by Christ, its divine author.

CHAPTER XIV.

Sinless Condition of the Resurrection Life. Positive Testimony of Paul and Christ.

What we have shown concerning Man's Earthly Nature and his Heavenly Nature.—His Home on Earth and his Home in Heaven.—The Positive Teaching of the Apostle and Christ.—Man to be the Victor over Death and Sin and Pain.—The Opinions of leading Writers on this Theme.

IN pursuing the grand theme of a Heaven for all God's great family in the world of light and glory, we have shown,

1. That man does not, and *cannot* possess the same constitutional nature in the future life that he has in this existence.

2. That a change of worlds necessitates a change of bodies—the future body being pure, spiritual, beautiful, immortal and glorious.

3. And an equally radical change must take place in *all* the elements of his nature, the resurrection being not simply a lifting up of the creature out of the mortal into immortality; out of the earthly into the heavenly, but out of the imperfect into the perfect; out of the condition of weakness, frivolity and sinfulness of our imperfect condition in this world, into the strength and holiness and completeness of a purely heavenly and divine state.

4. All this we endeavored to show to be true, reasoning from analogy. And,

5. These views we strengthened by contrasting the present imperfect physical brain with the future perfect spiritual structure that man will possess in the higher life, for the habitation of the soul, and through which the soul will have opportunity to develop itself, unfettered by the clogs of the flesh, forever and ever.

As indicated in the closing words of the preceding chapter, we would now further present the plain and positive testimony not only of the apostle, but of our dear Lord himself, to the effect that sin will not and *cannot* be a concomitant of man's nature in the resurrection life, but that it will be utterly absent from that existence. We do this that those who admit the instructions of the Bible to be the truth of God, but who at the same time treat the views we have presented in these pages with derision, may see how distinctly and positively God sanctions what they condemn.

First, it is admitted by all Christians that Paul in the 15th chapter of his letter to the Corinthian church, to which we have repeatedly referred in these pages, was treating of man's literal resurrection from this world into another. Now let the reader carefully examine for himself the instruction of the apostle, and he will find the following to be true. After declaring, as we have seen, that man dies in a condition of corruption, dishonor, weakness and with a mortal body, but is raised in a condition of incorruption, glory, power and with a spiritual body, he exclaims:—

"So WHEN this corruptible shall have put on incorruption, and this mortal shall have put on immortality, THEN shall be brought to pass the saying that is written, death is swallowed up in victory. O, death, where is thy sting? O, grave, where is thy victory?" He then immediately adds—"The sting of death is *sin*, and the strength of sin is the law, but thanks be to God which giveth us the victory through our Lord Jesus Christ." *

In all the Bible there is no Scripture which contains truth more glorious than this, or which should be regarded as of greater interest and importance to mankind. First it proclaims the absolute and positive destruction and end of *death*, through the power of the resurrection, and man's complete triumph over the grave. "*When* this corruptible shall have put on incorruption, and this mortal shall have put on immortality;"—in other words, when the soul of a man—or the man himself, which is the same thing—shall throw off his corrupt nature, and put on the incorruptible and immortal,—"THEN shall be brought to pass [or fulfilled] the saying [or promise] that is written, † death is swallowed up IN VICTORY!" The meaning of which is, in the resurrection, death is destroyed utterly! An end is made

---
* 1 Cor. 25:54-57.
† Isaiah 25.

of it. It shall never more hold dominion over man. With him, "there shall be no more death!" And second, in like manner it declares the utter destruction of sin, and man's complete victory over it, at the same moment death is destroyed. See how plain the apostle's instruction on this point. He makes man to exult in the resurrection life, and in his great joy to cry out, "O, death, where is thy sting?" Which is simply declaring that whatever he meant by the "sting of death," it was no where to be found in the resurrection life. It was utterly absent from that condition. It no longer held man in its power and led him captive at its will.

And we bless God that the Apostle has not left us in conjecture relative to *what he meant* by the "sting of death," for he immediately adds,—"The sting of death is SIN." So that the expression here must mean this,—that in the resurrection life there can be not only no such thing as *death*, but no such thing as *sin*. "O, death, where is thy sting?" This phrase, stripped of all figure and redundant verbiage, means simply this, nothing more nor less,— where is sin? As much as to say, it cannot be found! It no longer exists! It *was* a thing of the other life. *There* it ravaged and destroyed as did death. But it enters not into this world of spiritual purity. Christ is "the resurrection and the life." He is the end not only of death but of sin. These have dominion over all men, and swallow up all men in the world of sin and death; and then, God, through Christ, is represented as *swallowing them up* IN VICTORY! Immortality gulps them down, so that not a trace of them shall be known in the world of spirituality during the boundless ages of eternity! Hence the joyful exclamation of the apostle:—"Thanks be to God who giveth us the victory [over death and sin] through our Lord Jesus Christ!"

Here is the plain and emphatic teaching of the apostle relative to the subject under consideration. By it, the doctrine is clearly and positively taught that in the resurrection life there is no sin. Either this is true, or the apostle was deceived, for if in the future life, any soul in all the domain of spirituality can point to *any* place, *above* or *beneath*, or in any dark corner,—if there be a dark corner in that life,—and say in answer to the affirmative question of the apostle, "Where is sin, the sting of death?"—"There it is," or "*there*," or "THERE IS SIN," does not the reader perceive that the declaration of the apostle in the above words, would be simply false, for sin would exist where he affirms it does not,—and hence the instruction of the entire chapter which treats alone of the sublime subject of the resurrection, and is the source of so great consolation to millions, would be utterly unworthy their credence, and hence destitute of the very element of faith with which it now thrills the soul of the trustful believer!

How grand the theme as presented by the apostle! How worthy a God of infinite goodness, and how comforting to the soul! Why deny this glorious truth by saying that man in the future world will possess all the imperfections of this life with the same moral character, and that he can only realize the condition of sinlessness described by the apostle in the foregoing Scripture, after long ages,—perhaps millions of years of conflict with sin and wrong and error? Or go further, and, as do the mass of Christians, *eternalize* and *immortalize* SIN, the serpent—the devil—and make *him* the conqueror,—when it was the devil and all his works that Christ came into the world to crush and destroy, and over which the apostle declares he [Christ] should become the universal and glorious victor,—as the whole race of human intelligences should be "made *alive* IN *him!*"

See how plain his words:—"As in Adam all die, even so *in Christ* shall all be made alive. [And to be alive IN *Christ* is to be a new creature.] Then cometh the end when he shall have delivered up the kingdom to God, even the Father, when he shall have put down all rule and all authority and power. For he must reign till he hath put all enemies under his feet. The last enemy that shall be destroyed is death. And when all things shall be subdued unto him. then shall the Son also himself be subject unto Him that put all things under him, that GOD MAY BE ALL IN ALL."[*]

---
[*] 1 Cor. 15:24-27.

Thus is God, the loving Father, and not the devil, to become the victor over sin and death through Christ. And the apostle plainly assures us *when* all this shall be. It is not after man shall have existed long ages in *hades*,—or purgatory,—in a condition of sin and moral pollution, as in this life, but when he puts off his "earthly," "mortal," "corrupt" nature, and is born out of his condition of flesh and sin into the future immortal existence: —"So *when* this corruptible shall put on incorruption, and this mortal shall have put on immortality, *then* shall be brought to pass [or fulfilled] the *saying that is written, death is swallowed up in victory;*" and then it is that the sting of death which is sin shall be forever destroyed.

"The saying that is written." If we turn to the words of the prophet* and the context, we shall find him describing the grand consummation of the Gospel, under Christ, when "the Lord of hosts shall make unto *all people* a feast of fat things, a feast of wines on the lees, of fat things full of marrow, of wines on the lees well refined." *Then* "the face of the covering cast over all people" and "the vail" of unbelief and sin spread over all nations "shall be destroyed, and Christ shall swallow up death in victory, and the Lord God will wipe away tears from off all faces," for the Lord God had declared, or promised it!

Here is the sublime and glorious consummation

---
* Isaiah 25:7.

of the Gospel as foretold and described by the prophet, to which the apostle referred in his extended discussion on the resurrection, and the future immortal life, in his letter to the Corinthians, the fulfillment of which he here so vividly describes and applies to the condition of man in his resurrection life. As we have seen, he can never more be a subject of death or sin, as the apostle declares in his letter to the Romans:—"He that is dead is free from sin."* It is because he no longer possesses a "corruptible" nature. He is *sown* in corruption, but *raised* in incorruption." This admits of no sin in the resurrection, but points to the glorious time foretold by the revelator when in an ecstatic vision, he "saw a new Heaven and a new earth,"—and heard a great voice from Heaven, saying:—"Behold the tabernacle of God is with men, and He will dwell with them, and they shall be His people, and God Himself shall be with them and be their God. And God shall wipe away all tears from their eyes; and there *shall be no* MORE DEATH, *neither sorrow nor crying,* neither SHALL THERE BE ANY MORE PAIN, *for the former things have passsed away!"* †

Thanks to God, for this comforting truth!

<blockquote>
No aching hearts are there,
No tear-dimmed eye, no form by sickness wasted;
No cheek grown pale through penury or care;
No spirits crushed beneath the woes they bear,
No sighs for bliss untasted.
</blockquote>

---

* Rom. 6:7.
† Rev. 21:3-4.

No sad farewell is heard,
  No lonely wail for loving ones departed,
  No dark remorse is there o'er memory stirred,
  No smile of scorn, no harsh or cruel word
    To grieve the broken-hearted.

No long, dark night is there,
  No light from sun or silvery moon is given,
  But Christ, the Lamb of God, all bright and fair,
  Illumes the city with effulgence rare,
    The glorious light of Heaven!

And now, before we conclude this chapter, we must show how plainly and positively Christ himself authoritatively establishes the truth of all we have set forth in these pages relative to the sinless condition of man in the resurrection life. By referring to his controversy with the Sadducees,* the reader will find them making the same mistake relative to this subject as do the millions in our time,— viz., that the idea of a future life necessarily involves the existence in the other world of the same feelings, passions and desires experienced in this; and hence the question asked him relative to whose wife the woman should be in the spiritual life, who had seven husbands while living in the flesh.

Christ confutes the idea they entertained by the following positive and distinct annunciation:—

"Jesus answered and said unto them, 'Ye do err, not knowing the Scriptures, nor the power of God. For in the resurrection they neither marry nor are given in marriage, but are as the angels of God in Heaven, neither can they die any more; for they

---

* Math. 22, Mark 12, and Luke 20 chapters.

are equal unto the angels, and are children of God, being children of the resurrection.'"

Can language be plainer, or a declaration be framed more comforting and hopeful? By the phrase, "in the resurrection," Christ meant to designate the existence of man,—all men,—in the other life, and he plainly affirms that in that existence men will be no longer under the control of their worldly, sensual appetites and passions, but being purely spiritual, like the angels, they will have only spiritual desires.*

We find our own commentators † giving it as their opinion that these words of our dear Lord mean all we here represent, while the Rev. T. B. Thayer, D. D., in the work ‡ to which we have before referred, argues the subject at length, as below. We afford the reader the pleasure of perusing his views in his own language, rather than our representation of what he says on the subject, because of its clear and decided tone, and also because we wish him to see what are the thoughts of some of the leading men of our church on this great question. He says:—

"The second refers to their ignorance of the power of God so to change and adapt mankind to the Heavenly existence, as to avoid the difficulties they

---

* "Libertines of all sorts can form no idea of *Heaven* as a place of *blessedness*, unless they can hope to find in it the gratification of their sensual lusts. On this very ground Mohammed built his paradise."— Dr. A. Clark on Math. 22.

† Rev. L. R. Paige, D. D., and Rev. S. Cobb, D. D.

‡ "Theology of Universalism."

had started regarding the woman with seven husbands.

"The Sadducees fell into the common error, common even in our own time, that there is no change after death, that we carry with us into the future world the feelings, preferences and characteristics of this world; that what we desire here, we shall desire there, and what we do here, we shall continue to do there.

"All this the Savior positively and plainly denies, and shows that such reasoning is false, that the law of analogy does not hold to this extent; because this life is earthly and that will be heavenly; this life is in a material body, and that will be in a spiritual body. The difference in character and condition, in desires and pursuits, in the elements which go to make up our happiness, will be equally great. In this world we are mortal,—in that, we shall die no more. In this world we are men, subject to all the frailties and infirmities of human nature;—in that world, we shall be as the angels, children of God, because children of the resurrection. In this world, we are under the influence of the desires, the passions, the love of self, which characterize the flesh,—in that we shall be freed from these, and acknowledge the love, the law and dominion of the spirit; the conflict between the flesh and the spirit being forever at an end.

"The expression 'children of God, being children of the resurrection,' has immense weight in it. It is a direct assertion of the fact that the change wrought by the resurrection is moral and spiritual, and transforms the subject of it into the Divine likeness. The phrase 'son of' or 'children of' is a Hebrew form of speech, signifying, among other things, 'in the likeness of,' 'similar to,' 'resembling.'

"Now the Savior says that the resurrection works such an entire change in man, so purifies and exalts his soul, lifts him so entirely out of the earthly into the heavenly, that he becomes by this very *anastasis* or transformation, a child of God. Of course this establishes the fact that the resurrection has to do with more than the body. It is growth to the soul, enlightenment, instruction, education; and, through these, the lifting it up, leading it up, helping it rise up, into that spiritual perfection, that 'image of the heavenly,' reaching which it becomes the child of God in the highest and divinest meaning of the term. We are children of God in this sense, being, or *because* we are children of the resurrection; or in words of the same import, to be in the likeness of the resurrection is to be in the likeness of God.

"All the other phraseology is to the same point. The Savior is explicit and direct beyond mistake, and beyond controversy. The children of the resurrection are 'equal unto the angels,' they 'are as the angels which are in Heaven,' or 'as the angels of God in Heaven.' Now, these varied forms of expression are only so many ways of saying that, when the resurrection has completed its work on man, he becomes angelic. Can anything be more conclusive in evidence of the fact that the change is a moral and spiritual one? that it is a result brought about by moral and spiritual agencies, through which the soul is corrected, informed and raised up to Heaven, and 'changed into the same image, from glory to glory, even as by the spirit of the Lord?' "*

Such are the views of a leading divine of our church and one of the ablest theologians living, relative to the teachings of Christ concerning the subject under consideration. Can anything be more clear and explicit, or more grand and beatific? The more we reflect upon this sublime theme and what it contemplates for man in the glorious hereafter, the more profound is our gratitude to God, and the more is our soul filled with praise to His holy name.

"Oh, is there a thought in the wide world, so sweet,
  As that God has so cared for us, bad as we are,—
That he thinks of us, plans for us, stoops to entreat,
  And follows us, wander we ever so far?

"Then how can the heart e'er be drooping or sad,
  Which God hath once touched with the light of His grace?
Can the child have a doubt who but lately hath laid
  Himself to repose in the Father's embrace?

"And is it not wonderful, O, creature of God,
  That he should have honored us so with His love,—
That the sorrows of life should but shorten the road
  Which leads to Himself and the mansions above?"

---

* 1 Cor. 3:18.

CHAPTER XV.

Popular Views of our Moral and Spiritual Condition shown to be Errors.

Men say that Dying is simply throwing off one's Physical Body, like casting aside his garments, or like Passing from one Room into another.—These Ideas shown to be Errors.—The Beauty and Glory of our Future Home in Heaven when compared with our Life Here.—The Conditions of the Heavenly World all favorable to our Purity and Growth.—Comforting Thoughts from an Eminent Writer.

WE have now shown, we trust beyond doubt or cavil, from both Scripture and the teachings of reason and of nature, something of what must be the radical change in man by a change of worlds, through the death of our natural bodies and the resurrection of man himself, into a new form of being and condition of existence. And equally plain must it be, we think, to all reflecting minds, that those are in error who declare, as they often do to us, that "dying is simply throwing off one's physical body as a man would cast aside his garments, leaving his soul or the man in precisely the same moral and spiritual condition and under the same moral influences as when in the flesh." And also that "passing from one room into another, cannot change the character, or moral condition of a man, and *this is all the change that is produced* by *a change of worlds.* We shall be precisely the same beings in a moral sense in the future life that we are in this."

This assumption, we are aware, looks very plausible, but yet on a moment's reflection any one can see that its truth is simply impossible. Suppose a man dies a bald Atheist, with no belief in a God, Christ or a future life. In the resurrection he believes in all these. Can he be precisely the same man morally and spiritually he is in this life? Then if a change of worlds produces no more change in us than the bare stepping from one "room into another," it follows indubitably, that if a man is a drunkard before death, he will be a drunkard after death, and possess the character of a drunkard; if he is lewd, lascivious and a libertine before death, or a liar, a cheat, a knave, a thief, a robber or a murderer, he will be lewd, lascivious, a libertine, a liar, a cheat, a knave, a thief, a robber or murderer in the other world. Indeed, all the passions and lusts of the flesh to which he is subject here, must exist with him and influence him there, or it is impossible that he should *be the same man morally, there as here!*

Who can believe this. Men and women who regard themselves as specially fitted for Heaven, undoubtedly anticipate that immediately on passing "over the river," *they* will enjoy the delights that flow out from the *purity* and *glory* of the divine life. And yet let them look within their own hearts and take cognizance of the nest of lusts and passions that swarm there, and manifest themselves from time to time. Why will not these exist in *their* nature in the other world as well as in the natures of other sinners, for all are sinners in this life?

But *is* the changing of worlds like a "man casting aside his garments," or "merely passing out of one room into another?" We are anxious for all our readers candidly to consider this assumption, which is getting to be exceedingly fashionable with many "progressive Christians." Are the two cases at all parallel? All must see on a moment's consideration how the matter stands. The declaration relative to the two rooms is based upon the supposition that the two rooms are precisely similar and that the man destitute of his mortal body with its gross appetites, propensities and passions, and clothed upon with his pure, spiritual, celestial vestments,—as we are assured in the New Testament he will be in the resurrection,—experiences no more change in his feelings, views, propensities, passions, affections and aspirations, than does the man who simply casts aside his garments, as he retires for slumber. But how erroneous is this assumption and therefore false the idea predicated on the illustration. Every man is entirely conscious that, notwithstanding the *soul is the man*, and is the responsible agent in all moral actions, how constantly he is influenced by the lusts, appetites and passions of his physical nature, as we have shown in former chapters. Now if by death he throws off this bodily garment, *and the resurrection clothes him with one precisely similar,* then we grant that the illustration adduced, bears some resemblance to the thing to which it is applied. But this is not true. In changing worlds, the soul is not only deprived by death of its old, imperfect, mortal garment, whose influence is to sin and corruption, but it is clothed upon by the resurrection with its *spiritual, immortal and glorious robes of celestial beauty and purity.*

So of the two rooms, and the passage from the one into the other. *This* is a world of darkness, coldness, ignorance, sin, hatred, emulation, wrath, strife, envying, malice, disappointment, sorrow, suffering, despair and so on to the end of the dark chapter. All these, we know, exist in this life, while we remain connected with the flesh. Surrounding us on every hand are objects to tempt the soul astray. Both within and without do we find elements of impurity. Through the eye, the ear, by the taste and the touch and all the senses, is the soul tempted. *Why* we were so created and so surrounded, by a God of infinite goodness and wisdom, we cannot explain, only on the hypothesis that he designed our existence here to be one of imperfection, trial, discipline, to be followed by one of perfection, purity, knowledge, glory.

And this is our belief, founded on the plain teachings of the New Testament. The "room," or world into which we shall be ushered through the portals of death and a glorious resurrection, shall not be similar to this, thanks to God! *There*, no darkness or deformity, or sickness or temptation or any of the appetites, imperfections and evils mentioned above, as connected with the flesh, shall exist. We appeal to the Scriptures, and challenge contradiction. The future life is one of pure spirituality. It is a world resplendent with all that is divine, beatific and glorious. It hath no need of the sun or the moon to shine in it, for the glory of God doth lighten it and the Lamb is the light thereof.

It is typified as Eden, where the glow of an eternal summer smiles, and unfading flowers bloom; where trees whose leaves never wither, impart a cooling shade, and the glow of perpetual verdure, and the fragrance of celestial bowers, forever delight the soul. It is called Paradise, and is represented as creation's "Holy of Holies." There, no man is "drawn away of his own lusts and enticed." There, he exists not for ages in ignorance and rags. There, he will not be tempted by starvation, nor by any innate desire, to steal or kill, nor to be drunken by a fleshly appetite, nor to acts of lewdness and profligacy by physical passions. He will not be surrounded by persons of depraved natures to lead him astray, or to deceive, degrade and destroy him.

Oh! no, only spiritual beings shall form his companionship. Angels of purity and beauty shall instruct, educate and lead him. In short, all the influences by which he shall be surrounded and guided shall be holy and elevating. He shall live in and breathe only an atmosphere of love. This is the element of the celestial world; the breath of its inhabitants,—the language by which they commune, —the all-pervading power that harmonizes their souls and makes them one; the radiance that beams from their eyes as they look with delight upon each other! This shall be the nature and character of our Home in Heaven!

> "That world to come! and O how blest!—
> Fairer than prophets ever told;
> And never did an angel-guest
> One-half its blessedness unfold.
>
> "It is all holy and serene.—
> The land of glory and repose;
> And there, to dim the radiant scene,
> No tear of sorrow ever flows.
>
> "It is not fanned by summer gale;
> 'Tis not refreshed by vernal showers
> It never needs the moon-beam pale,
> For there are known no evening hours.
>
> "There forms unseen by mortal eye,
> Too glorious far our sight to bear,
> Are walking with their God on high,
> And waiting our arrival there."

Yes, we believe with the poet, that so much purer and more beautiful and glorious is the world of spirituality into which we shall be ushered than this, that were we translated instantly into that existence, with our present bodily organs, we could no more gaze upon the radiance of celestial forms and faces and the wonderful splendor of that world, than could the Jews upon the countenance of Moses when arrayed in the lustre of God; or could Saul of Tarsus upon the glowing brightness which shone round and about him from Christ who met him in the way and whose effulgence, though he saw no man, was so overpowering as to prostrate him to the earth.

These are our views of the condition of the celestial life and the great difference there is between the present and future worlds;—the "room" we now occupy, and that into which we shall pass when this mortal shall put on immortality, and this dishonorable, the glorious!

Can it be, then, that changing worlds is simply throwing off this physical body as a man would cast off his garments to lie down to sleep? Or, that it is merely like passing from one room into another of the same character in the same dwelling, leaving him precisely the same being morally and spiritually?

In the light of the foregoing reflections, we can see but one way in which these questions can be answered. Death will divest us of our earthly robe. That is true. But with it will go our *earthly nature*, and we shall be invested with a nature more spiritual and divine! *That* is also true. How, then, can we be precisely the same creatures morally and spiritually in the other life we are in this?

Instead of this, our nature, our opportunities, all our tendencies, will be different;—more exalted and divine. A leading orthodox clergyman,* in a ser-

---
* Rev. Henry Ward Beecher.

mon, while dwelling on this subject, truthfully says:

"There is a strong tendency manifested among men at this time to make the other life an absolute and literal continuation of this. 'Just as a man goes out of this, just so he begins in the other world,' they say. This is not so.

"We shall enter upon another life divested of many of the hindrances and incumbrances of this. When we pass from life, we shall leave behind, not only the body, but all that part of the passions and the appetites which has its function and sphere on account of our poor, bodily condition. It seems to me that much that mars life is what we call infirmity; and that when we die, we leave behind us many things that we call faults and foibles, and sins, as the trees shed their leaves when winter comes. When the body dies, oh! how much will perish that is the result of the forces of those passions which sleep with the flesh! When we go from this world, how shall we be released from ten thousand things that belong to our physical state, and that tend to hinder our spiritual development."

That is true; and it is also true that the world into which we shall go will have a tremendous power over the soul in developing its divine nature, which can never be known or experienced in this life. On this subject the author from whom we have just quoted, says again in a sermon on Death, which is full of cheering, comforting thoughts:—

"If you take a seed that has ripened in Nova

Zembla, and bring it into the tropics and plant it, it will not be what it would have been in Nova Zembla, with a short growing season, and the scantiest supply of food. It will have, with a long summer and an abundant supply, a growth to which no one would suspect that it could attain, who had only seen it grow in the frigid zones. Many things that are shrubs in the frigid zones are high, waving century oaks in the tropics. And so men in this life are in conditions which, though fitted to develop the earlier stages of human growth, are not fitted to develop the full estate of that idea which God has expressed in the creation of man. And we may hope that when we bid adieu to our mortal life, we shall leave behind some things which are necessary to the exigencies of our condition here, but which will not be necessary to our state there. Our imagination, our reason, our affections and our moral sentiments, we shall doubtless carry with us; but the conditions of our life will be so different that we shall be like men taken from poverty into abundance; from winter into summer; from a cold climate and a frozen soil, into a soil never locked by ice, and skies that never know frost. Our life there will be ampler, fuller, nobler than it is here."

Yes, we shall no longer grope in ignorance, but shall see as face to face and know as we are also known. Knowledge of God, of His dear Son, of the purity and enjoyment of angels, of the extent and wonders of the universe, of the nature of the divine government, of the joys of love, and countless sources of improvement and spiritual delight, shall be received through the intuitive powers and perceptions of the nature we shall possess on entering the glorious temple above, and shall elevate and strengthen and bless every soul of the great family of God in that celestial world of light and love.

"One sweetly welcome thought
 Comes to me o'er and o'er,
1 am nearer home to-day
 Than I ever have been before.
Nearer my Father's house,
 Where the many mansions be,
Nearer the great white throne,
 Nearer the crystal sea;—

"Nearer that bound of life
 Where we lay our burdens down,
Nearer leaving the cross,
 Nearer gaining the crown.
Father, perfect my trust;
 Let my spirit feel in death
That her feet are firmly set
 On the rock of a living faith."

CHAPTER XVI.

Views of the Objector Considered.

The Objector may say that it still appears to him Men will Sin in the Other Life.—If so, what will be the Nature of the Sins he will Commit? —This Question should be Carefully Considered.—The Body the great Inciting Cause of Sin.—Hatred in the Soul not possible in the Heavenly Life.—Impossible for us to possess the same Characters in the Resurrection that we have Here.

TO what we have endeavored to establish as the wonderful truth of Christ in the Gospel, the objector may now say it still appears to him that, notwithstanding the facts we have adduced, man will sin in the future life and possess the same character there he has here. If the reader still entertains these feelings, let him imagine if he can, how man can sin if utterly destitute of a nature to sin, and in the entire absence of all temptation to sin! And above all, let him consider what will be *the nature* of the sins he will commit. We wish him to do this, not only to convince him that the future life is not one of enmity and wickedness, but to show him more clearly the superiority of our home in Heaven to our home on earth.

We ask the reader again to consider the question, if we sin in the other life, *what will be the nature of our sins?* Can he imagine? Shall we steal from our neighbor, or cheat him, or lie about him, or deceive him, or rob him, or be guilty of adultery, or drunkenness or murder? Does not the reader discover that several of these sins, if not all of them, will be impossible in a life of pure spirituality? The multiplied physical wants of our present existence, clamoring perpetually as they do for gratification, will be utterly unknown in the future life. Dwellings and clothing for the protection of our bodies, and food and drink to nourish them, and which, in this life, must, of necessity, be supplied, and often in great extravagance, demanding larger supplies of money than can be honestly furnished, will be absent entirely from that future and diviner world. Traffic will be unknown in that world as will the deception practiced by ten thousand methods in carrying it forward in this life. All know and acknowledge, that the soul while connected with the body is influenced to do wrong by the appetites and passions of the flesh. Shall we commit any of *these* sins? The apostle, in enumerating the evil deeds of men, —"adultery, fornication, uncleanness, hatred, variance, wrath, strife, * * and such like," "embracing," as Dr. Adam Clarke* affirms, "all evil passions, and every sin that the law of God specifies and condemns,"—defines them all as "*the works of the flesh.*"† This is not *our* language, nor declaration, but *that of inspiration.*

---

* Learned Commentator of the Methodist Church.

† Rev. S. Cobb, D. D., says in his comments on this passage :—"Paul here enumerates as the 'works of the flesh,' all descriptions of sin known

Now when our bodies shall have died and become the dust and rubbish of the grave, and our souls shall have been clothed upon with the "incorruption," spiritual "power" and "glory" of the heavenly world, shall we longer continue to do these works of the flesh or either of them? Shall we not then be lifted above, beyond and out of reach of them?

And if *not*, what then, we ask again, will be the *nature* or *character* of our sins? Will those who contend that we shall still exist in iniquity and indulge in crime and wickedness, inform us as to the nature of our iniquity, crime and wickedness? In what will it consist?

They may answer that "sin consists not so much in *outward acts* of wrong-doing as in hatred of the heart toward God and man." But this is the very *condition of soul* that the apostle describes in the above catalogue, "hatred," "wrath," etc., as belonging to the "*works of the flesh.*" By which he means that this enmity toward God and the principles of God's government,—also the appetites and passions of our nature which manifest themselves when not properly controlled, in the committal of the outward evil acts enumerated in this dark catalogue,—*belong to our existence in the flesh*. They do not reach into the spiritual and celestial life.

---

in the world. Not that the physical body is the responsible *sinner*," he continues, "for the higher nature which we call the mind, is the responsible child of God. But all the circumstances, the influences, the inducements and the temptations to sin *belong to and proceed from the animal nature in its earthly relations.*"—*Commentary on the New Testament.*

In that existence, having been divested of our physical being with all its lusts, appetites and passions, and being clothed upon with a new, spiritual vestment, pure and glorious, with the knowledge of God's character in all its beauty and purity, in our hearts, a condition of hatred in our souls will be impossible, as will sin in a nature where the element of sin or the desire to sin shall no longer exist. Let those who contend that we shall still be filled with wrath, malice and hatred toward God and each other in the resurrection, first gainsay the inspired testimony to which we have referred. Supposition and mere conjecture should weigh nothing against the plain and positive declarations of Him who "came to bring life and immortality to light," and who said that in the resurrection "they are as the angels of God."

But the objector still affirms, perhaps, that if men do not and cannot sin in the future life, they will possess the same *desire* to sin they have in this life, and, consequently, will carry the same sinful *characters* with them into the other existence they possess when they leave this. For instance, he says, by way of illustration, the drunkard has a strong innate appetite for intoxicating drink, a libertine, a passion for lewdness, a thief, a desire to steal, etc., —and further, that if these men should be confined each separately in a cell, they could commit none of these offences, but yet they would each still possess the same desires which existed in their natures while they were in a condition of freedom, and hence the drunkard would still be a drunkard in character, the thief a thief in character, etc. All of which we admit. If they still possessed the same sinful desires and inclinations, they would possess the same characters. But the objector takes these persons out of their physical bodies into the resurrection life and clothes them with immortal, incorruptible and spiritual vestments, and says *so it shall be with them in that new existence.* Men cannot become drunkards in the spirit world, but if they die drunkards they will have the character of the drunkard in that life. If they die libertines, they will have this character in the spiritual existence. If they die thieves, they will have the character of thieves, etc. They will be sinful in the elements of their nature though it will be impossible for them to commit the sins enumerated above, and others of a similar nature.

But never was reasoning more fallacious or unscriptural. Men affirm with great confidence and flipyancy that human beings will possess precisely the same characters in the future world they have in this existence. But do they consider the utter impossibility of the truth of their affirmation, and how entirely contrary to the plain declarations of the Scriptures it is? What is *"character"* as applied to man? Webster says "it is the sum of the *qualities* which distinguish one person from another." Consider now how largely the *passions*, *appetites* and *lusts* which are purely physical, enter into and help make up the *qualities* or *characteristics* that distinguish men one from another. These all belong exclusively to the flesh. They *sway* the minds of men, but are not elementary qualities of the soul, nor do they in any proper sense belong to the soul or are they "innate" in it. Now will any one have the hardihood to contend that these appetites, passions and lusts will exist in man and help make up his *character* in a purely spiritual existence in the resurrection life? One man is a glutton, another a drunkard, another a sensualist, in this life. These qualities belong to the flesh, will die with the body, and go with it into the grave. They will never be felt by the soul, nor influence the soul in the spiritual and divine existence beyond the grave, and hence the impossibilty of the truth of the declaration that men will possess the "same characters" in a heavenly existence, which they possess when they die.

Do men possess the same *characters* in this life after they have been renovated in their minds by the holy spirit in conversion so as to become new creatures? This is not possible, as all acknowledge. How, then, can a man possess the same character in a sinless condition, when born out of his body of lust and passion into one of spirituality and glory, being renewed in all his nature? This also is impossible!

And, we contend that in their very souls should men be glad, and thankful to God for this glorious truth. For if we were fated to be in the future world just what we are here, what a set of pigmies and sinful, selfish, wanton, envious, proud, disdainful, treacherous, hypocritical, ungodly wretches the purest and most saintly of men would find themselves to be! Oh! where is the man or the woman who does not *know* this to be true? And then see how plainly all this preposterous talk of our possessing the same moral qualities in the resurrection life is contradicted by the apostle, as we have repeatedly shown in these pages, where he so positively declares that the future life is one of "incorruptibility" and "glory;" and by Christ, who says that "in the resurrection they shall be as the angels of God," and in our glad deliverance from sin and death, we are made to exclaim by the apostle, "Thanks be to God who giveth us the victory through our Lord Jesus Christ!"

How can all this be, and still we be in possession of the same *characters* we have in this life? Do the angels possess sinful moral qualities? The reader will see how impossible is the supposition, and how utterly inconsistent it is with the plain teaching of the New Testament. The present imperfections of our nature will not be known in Heaven. It is a state of spiritual purity and celestial love and glory.

"There all around shall love us,
And we return their love;
One band of happy spirits,
One family above;

> And there no sin nor sorrow,
> Nor pain nor death is known;
> But pure, glad life, enduring
> As Heaven's benignant throne."

But it is objected again, that salvation is impossible without *regeneration*. Said Christ, "Marvel not that I said unto you, ye must be born again. It is true, Christ said this. But he nowhere affirms that spritual regeneration *before death* is indispensable to a resurrection into another life, or to a *happy* existence in another life. Indeed, no such intimation can be found in all the Bible. If this were true not one in ten thousand of the millions who people this earth would ever reach the abodes of heavenly bliss. And yet, Christ said, as above stated, "Marvel not that I said unto thee, ye must be born again."

And what, pray, have we advanced in these chapters that militates against this divine and elevating truth? Have we not shown, not only that regeneration is indispensable to salvation from sin and error, and all their dark catalogue of evils, disappointments and sorrows, but that the resurrection *is* regeneration;—the perfection of the "new birth,"—which by its transforming energy brings the soul into the "likeness of God," and so lifts it up into spiritual perfection that it becomes the "image of the heavenly," and the "child of God," in the highest and divinest meaning of the term. As Christ expresses it, they are thus "the children of God, and are as the angels, *because* they are the children of the resurrection." We do not believe that men go to Heaven *in* their sins. Heaven is freedom from sin. The resurrection liberates the soul from sin,—and so renovates and transforms it that it is "changed into the same image, from glory to glory, even by the spirit of the Lord."

> "Heaven is the land where troubles cease,
>   Where toils and tears are o'er;
> The blissful clime of rest and peace,
>   Where cares distract no more;
> And not the shadow of distress
> Dims its unsullied blessedness.
>
> "Heaven is the dwelling-place of joy,
>   The home of light and love,
> Where faith and hope in rapture die,
>   And ransomed souls above
> Enjoy, before the eternal throne,
> Bliss everlasting and unknown."

CHAPTER XVII.

Christ--The Object of his Mission.--Heir of all Things.--The Resurrection and the Life.

If the Doctrine advanced in these Pages be true, how is Christ the Savior of Men?—The Perfect Work of the Gospel not fully accomplished in this Life.—Pre-existence of Christ.—He is Heir of all Things.—The Head of every Man.—The Resurrection and the Life.—The Savior of the World.

WE have shown in preceding chapters that such is the nature of the change produced by the *anastasis*, or raising up of the soul in connection with its pure spiritual resurrection vestment, on the death of the physical body, that neither sin nor the desire to sin will longer exist as an element of our constitutional nature.

If all this is true, asks the objector,—if *death* or the *grave* saves us from sin, how can Christ be our Savior? But the reader misunderstands or mistakes when he supposes that *we* have advanced this view. We have not said or even *intimated* that *death* or the *grave* works the *change* to which we have referred, in a change of worlds, and we would be exceedingly glad if *all* our readers will do us the justice to endeavor to comprehend us and not misrepresent our position in this particular.

Death has no power to produce the new celestial body, or to exalt the soul in holiness and knowledge, or to afford *life* to the soul. It is opposed to life and can exist only where there is no life, and is simply a *negative condition*. It *is the cessation of life—organic* or *animal* life. The body which is dead *has no life in it.* That is all; and it is the extent of the influence of death. How absurd the idea that DEATH will affect the change *in man* described by Paul in the 15th chapter of Corinthians as the work of the resurrection *through the Lord and Savior Jesus Christ.* None but an idiot would harbor such a conception. Instead of this being true, death itself is to be destroyed through the very change to which we refer.

All the work of the Gospel revealed in the person and promises and acts of Christ. expressed by the significant word "*Salvation,*" is wrought through the spiritual energy, which, under Christ, has the power to "conquer death," "destroy it," yea "*swallow it up* IN VICTORY!"

God works *by means.* So far as the human race is concerned, Christ is their HEAD. He is "the head of *every* man." "The Father loveth the son and hath given all things into his hands." By which we are assured that the whole human race, under God, belongs to Christ. He is "heir of all things." Even the "heathen and the uttermost parts of the earth" are "his possession." "For to this end he hath died and rose and revived that he might be

Lord [possessor] of both the dead and the living." For what purpose has the entire possession and supervision of the *whole family of man* been bestowed by God upon His Son? We answer, that he might save them from sin, error and the grave, and impart to them the divine and glorious blessings which come to the soul through the truth and righteousness of his religion, and the delights and unspeakable glories of the immortal world. The Gospel everywhere represents all spiritual gifts and blessings and even the resurrection into another existence, though effected through natural laws, and *immortality* itself, as coming from God the Father, *through* the Lord and Savior Jesus Christ. He is the appointed agent in the hands of God, for the bestowment of these unspeakably glorious blessings. Men are saved, but not *fully* from sin and error in *this* life.

The "perfect work" of the Gospel is never accomplished in the present world, for notwithstanding the prevalence of the Gospel, and the professions of some men to sanctity, there is no man able to boast of *perfection*. We are all sinners in a certain sense, though we may have embraced Christ and believed on his name. We all *know* this to be true. Temptations are upon the right hand and the left, and we are liable to be "drawn away of our own lusts and enticed." The very best man on earth, is, at times, under the influence of sinful lusts or moved by a wrong spirit, let his professions be what they may, and can say in the language of Paul, "I find then a law that when I would do good, evil is present with me; for I delight in the law of God after the inward man; but I see another law in my members warring against the law of my mind, and bringing me into captivity to the law of sin which is in my members; O, wretched man that I am, *who shall deliver me from the body of this death;*" [literally this dead body—body of sin.] He answers, "I thank God *through* Jesus Christ our Lord. So with the mind I myself serve the law of God, but with the flesh, the law of sin." *

Here the apostle declares that he was brought into captivity to the law of sin which was in his members; and he moreover despairs of ever being entirely free from the lust of sin, till he is relieved of his body. "O, wretched man that I am, who shall deliver me from *this dead body?*" Saith an eminent commentator † in his lucid remarks on this passage :—"There seems to be here an allusion to an ancient custom of tyrants, who bound a *dead body* to a *living man*, and obliged him to carry it about." Paul regarded his body as a source of sin, through its appetites and lusts. And he desired to be *saved* or delivered from its corrupting influence. But could he *save himself?* No. He had embraced Christianity; the vail of ignorance—the *love* of sin, and the *fear* of death had been removed,

---
* Rom. 7:21-26.
† Rev. Adam Clarke. Methodist, on Rom. 7:24.

but still he was a *sinner*. The *full* and *perfect work* of the Gospel had not yet been accomplished. *So far*, he had been able to "work out" his "own salvation;" but he had now done all he could do; for he had no power to relieve himself of his body of flesh and clothe himself with garments of immortality. So he exclaimed, "Who shall deliver me from this dead body?" And the answer is, in substance, "The work shall be accomplished *through* the Lord Jesus Christ." Precisely so must it be with all men and all women.

Those who suppose that Christ has nothing to do with the work of the resurrection, in bringing the human family from the present state of sin into the future world of life, immortality and glory, have but a superficial view of this sublime subject. The whole is entrusted to him. He exclaims, "I am the resurrection and the life. I am he that liveth and was dead; and behold I am alive forevermore, and have THE KEYS of *hades* [the grave] and of death." Whatever the change to be effected for man, or however it is to be wrought out through the process of the resurrection, it is always ascribed to Christ, as the agent of God. Hence it is that everywhere in the New Testament we hear the expression from the early disciples to the effect that they expected to be raised "through Christ." That all should be "made alive *in* Christ." He exclaims, "The Father loveth the Son and hath given *all things* into his hands." Again he says, "All that the Father giveth me shall come to me and him that cometh to me I will in no wise cast out, for I came down from Heaven not to do mine own will, but the will of Him that sent me; and this is the Father's will who hath sent me, that of all which he hath given me I should lose nothing *but raise it up at the last day.*" "I go to prepare a place for you, so when I have prepared a place for you, *I will come again and receive you unto myself, that where I am, there ye may be also.*"

Has Christ then nothing to do with the glorious and sublime work of bringing the great family of man of whom he is the "Head" while they are "his members," from mortality into immortality, from the natural body into the spiritual, from weakness to power, from the dishonorable to the glorious? All this may be done and probably is, through what we call natural laws that govern the spiritual and physical of our being. Still, the work is in some way under the supervision of Christ, and committed to his charge. Even his own resurrection was a work of his own accomplishment. "Destroy this temple," said he, (speaking of his body,) "and in three days *I* will raise it up again." He did not affirm that *God* would do the work, or that it would be self-accomplished, but it would be effected through his own instrumentality.

The objector may here say that this view leaves out of the account the millions upon millions who lived and died previous to Christ's existence. For four thousand years men were born and died, and were destitute of a Savior, and hence, according to this theory there was no resurrection because there was no Christ, and men went into their graves and there they remain to this day, in dust and pollution.

But this objection is based on the assumption that Christ had no existence and the world no Savior *till Jesus made his appearance on earth.* But we do not so read and interpret the sacred Word. He had existence just as really before he came to our earth as he now has; and was just as much the Savior of man as he now is. The Bible declares that "he is the beginning of the creation of God" [spiritual creation]. He said:—"*I came forth from my Father* and am come into the world; again, I leave the world and *go to my Father.*" Again he says: —"I came down *from Heaven* not to do," etc. And again:—"Now Father glorify Thou me with Thine own self, *with the glory* I HAD WITH THEE BEFORE THE WORLD WAS."

On another occasion, he said directly to the Jews who had been boasting that they had Abraham to their father:—"*Before Abraham was, I am.*" * By which he meant that his existence had its origin before Abraham was born. He did not say that his existence was from eternity, or that he was co-existent with the Almighty, but that his existence dated anterior to that of Abraham, who lived two thousand years before Christ's incarnation.

The whole connection in which this declaration

---
* John 8:58.

was made, is interesting and instructive. He said to the Jews:—"Verily, verily, I say unto you, if a man keep my sayings he shall never see death." That is, he shall not die in verity and such shall be the nature of his faith, he shall not *expect* to die. For a man with *such* a faith, the death of his body shall have no terrors. He will feel that, on its dissolution, *he* shall depart and gain his heavenly home and be with Jesus, which is far better than to remain in the flesh.

"Then the Jews said unto him, now we know that thou hast a devil. Abraham is dead and the prophets, and thou sayest, if a man keep thy sayings he shall never taste of death."

"Art thou greater than our father Abraham who is dead?" As if they had said, "Abraham kept God's saying, and yet he died."—"Art thou greater than he? Whom makest thou thyself?"

"Jesus answered, it is my Father that honoreth me. I know Him. * * Your father Abraham rejoiced to see my day. He saw it and was glad."

"Then said the Jews unto him, thou art not yet fifty years old, and hast thou seen Abraham?"

"Then said Jesus unto them, before Abraham was I am." As if he had said, "Of course I have seen him. My existence dates prior to his. I knew him on earth. I have known him in Heaven; and he has seen me and rejoiced in the work entrusted to my care, of destroying death, raising the human race to immortal blessedness, of *bringing a knowl-*

edge of this glorious consummation down to this world of ignorance where the souls of men are all their lifetime subject to bondage through fear of death."

For ourself, we believe that Christ had existence in the spirit world even before the creation of the first man. "As in Adam all die, even so in Christ shall all be made alive." This is retrospective, as well as prospective. It runs back and includes the first man, and forward and embraces the whole world. Adam was "made alive *in Christ*" not four thousand years subsequent to the death of his body, but immediately after, just as any man in our day is made alive in Christ by the resurrection power delegated to Christ, and the transforming birth through which he passes into the higher existence. So of all who have since lived on earth and passed away. Jesus is the "Alpha and Omega," and "Lord both of the dead and the living, *for all live unto him*."— He is declared to be "The head of every man." Hence, it requires every man of the great family of God to constitute the body of which Christ is the head. And thanks to God, the body must follow its head.

"Where should the living body be,
But with the Living Head."

All who died were made alive *in* Christ; raised up to Heaven and glory. Hence, Christ was no stranger to the old patriarchs. He met Moses and Elias on the mount of transfiguration. It was not their *first* meeting. Perhaps the meeting was by appointment. Any one would so infer from the account given. Our blessed Master did not ascend the mountain without a purpose. Some suppose that all who had died before Christ came into the world, were still in *hades*, or hell, and that Christ visited them after his death upon the cross, for the first time. But we believe they were in a spiritual and exalted, heavenly condition, with Christ and Moses and Elias. Christ said to the malefactor upon the cross, when in the agony of death :—"To-day shalt thou be with me in Paradise." In our Lord's absence from his body, he was not in any *purgatory*, but in a condition of spirituality and celestial happiness, where perhaps he again greeted the old patriarchs whom he had seen but a short time before, in the presence of his disciples on the mount. How sublime the description of this wondrous scene! Christ was transfigured before his disciples. His face did shine as the sun, his raiment was white as the light, while a brilliant cloud enveloped the spiritual forms of Moses and Elias. All this was to give the disciples some faint conception of the wonderful purity, delight and glory of the heavenly existence. Then came the declaration from out of the cloud, "This is my beloved Son in whom I am well pleased [in whom I delight], hear ye him." That is, harken to his voice;—abide by his requirements, and confide in his promises of another and more glorious life.

With all who believe that Christ holds the keys of the grave, death is abolished through faith. And whether men feel the loving influence of Christ's power and blessed spirit in this life or not, he is their great spiritual head—they are his body. Under his supervision shall they be raised to another existence, and there, if not in this life, freed from the corruption of the flesh, shall be brought into perfect agreement with his divine and heavenly spirit, and be fully and forever saved.

From all this it will be seen how broad and grand is the theme of Christian salvation as applied to our race. It includes the world. It will be seen, too, how intimately and lovingly the Lord Jesus Christ, the Son of the living God, is connected with this work and how God himself has pledged His word for its accomplishment. With all those who believe that Christ holds the keys of the grave, death is abolished through faith. What an unspeakable blessing! "Ye who have *believed do* enter into rest!" And what a "rest" is this for the soul! Rest that springs from an unshaken faith in the cheering truth that the dear ones gone still live, and live in a world of purity, spirituality and delight, and that we shall go to them, and know them and with increased knowledge of God and our enjoyments enhanced, we shall mingle in the society of the Redeemed forever. How resplendent is the light which is thus sent down from the world of celestial beauty into the valley of death. We weep at the thought of their absence, but what joy in the reflection that their happiness and their love are now perfect and immortal. For a boon so precious how we should feel to praise the great Being from whom all blessings flow.

"Beautiful home of life and light,
Thy glory beams upon our sight;
Thy anthems ring from dome to dome,
Home of the angels, happy home.

"Over thy radiant bending skies,
The hues of morning float and rise;
Gently, as breathes the voice of prayer,
Songs of the sinless fill the air.

"Beautiful home of love divine,
Our deepest hearts around thee twine;
Unto thy summer bowers we come,
Home of the angels, HAPPY HOME!"

CHAPTER XVIII.

Conditions of our Heavenly Home Considered and Questions Answered.

Shall all stand on an Equality in the Future Life?—Can there be Progression There?—Shall we feel accountable to God and under the same obligations to Love and Serve Him we do in this Life, and will all be equally happy There?—Infinite Diversity both Here and Hereafter.—Sublime Truths concerning Heaven.

WE have shown in these pages that such will be the change wrought in the whole being of man by a change of worlds, through the power and process of the resurection, that in the future he will possess a constitutional nature which shall be destitute of sinful desires, passions, propensities and inclinations. The lusts of the flesh will no longer constitute an element of his nature; nor will he be moved by the impulse of hatred, enmity and revenge as in this existence. This life is earthly; the future will be heavenly. Here we inhabit material bodies; in the future our entire being will be spiritual. Here we possess an element which is mortal; in the future, mortality will be swallowed up of life. Here, all men sin; in the future, the desire to sin, the temptation to sin, and sin itself will be eradicated from our natures and be unknown to all forever. All this we think we have clearly shown from the teaching of the divine Word, and also from a correct philosophy.

The questions may now be asked, if the writer is correct in the sentiments advanced, will not all stand on a perfect equality on their entrance into the spiritual life? Will there be progression there? Shall we feel accountable to God and under the same obligations there to love and serve Him that Christians do here? And shall we, or shall we not, all be alike happy there? These are interesting questions. They are involved in the general subject under consideration, and are often asked by those whose minds are not quite clear relative to the principles which they illustrate.

In briefly offering our views upon them, we would premise what we have to say, by reminding the reader of the fact that the writer's conclusions are drawn from what appears to him to be legitimate necessities in the nature of things, rather than from any definite instruction he can obtain from the revealed Word relative to the general subject. The Bible is almost entirely silent concerning it. People generally suppose that the views of the Resurrection and the other life, presented in these chapters, necessitate a perfect equality in all respects among the great family of God's children in the celestial existence. That there can be no progression in that life,—that all will be equally happy, and that on their entrance into Heaven their happiness will be the highest possible that celestial beings can enjoy. And they present this consideration, in the spirit of ridicule, as an unanswerable objection to the system which we have advocated, as the truth of the Scriptures, strengthened and supported by the teachings of nature.

But we wish to say distinctly here that the objector mistakes when he supposes that the views we have presented necessitate any such conclusions as he describes. This will appear by the consideration of a few facts intimately connected with the general subject. And,

1. How can all persons stand on an equality in all respects on their entrance into the future existence, when some enter as infants, others in the vigor of manhood, others in old age, others in ignorance, others who were idiots in this world, and others still who were educated? Some enter as full grown Christians, and others with no knowledge of God, and no spiritual culture and discipline.

With some, all the circumstances of their lives on earth, from the cradle to the grave, and all their surroundings are unfavorable to moral growth. They are "conceived in iniquity and brought forth in sin," and as soon as they are capable of learning anything, are instructed in the arts of deception and the practice of vice. Those who have visited the Five Points, New York, and studied what they saw, know to what we refer. On the other hand, with millions, all the circumstances of their existence here are favorable to their moral, spiritual and intellectual advancement. Their parents are pure-minded, wealthy, highly cultured, religious, and, in every respect, qualified, not only to watch over their offspring with care and assiduity, but to educate them into a love of all that is divine, moral, pure, noble, spiritual and elevating. In the condition we have described, we will suppose the bodies of both these classes die, at which time, or immediately after, they —by which we mean their spirits—are resurrected out of their bodies of lust and passion and made *equally* partakers of celestial purity. But how can this possibly put them upon a condition of perfect equality as to knowledge? Those who die infants or idiots, in the resurrection life, as we have seen, will possess just as perfect minds and spiritual bodies as the educated; but to say they will be in possession of knowledge and experience equal to minds cultured by long years of study and discipline, is to assert what is exceedingly improbable if not *impossible*. Hence *we* do not believe they *"will* stand on a perfect equality," only in relation to the *element* or *substance* of their being. What will constitute the essense of their existence will be *spiritual* and *pure* with one as well as another. "It is sown in corruption, it is raised in *incorruption.*" So says the apostle. Hence it follows, that in this one respect,—that is, in the substance of their being,—all men will stand on a perfect equality; but in many others things they will not stand on an equality. Millions in this life were in ignorance of God, of their Savior, of the philosophy of nature, and of the wonders and glories of the universe. And now they have entered upon a diviner life, but on their first entrance, they have had no opportunity for any great advancement in the knowledge of these things; or, at all events, no greater opportunity than others, and must, therefore, occupy somewhat the same position, *relatively*, as it regards the other class, they did while in the flesh.

To be sure, all wrong desires and every inclination and propensity to evil, have been eradicated from their nature, and they experience only the impulses and promptings which come from the pure and holy elements of their new and exalted existence, and are all alike made capable of receiving knowledge intuitively, or otherwise, and will *feel* their divine and heavenly elevation. But when compared with the other class whose circumstances of birth and surroundings had been favorable to a higher condition of culture and discipline in this life, they cannot be their equals.

What a difference on their entrance into the higher life, between a Newton and an ignorant savage, in the degree of their intelligence of the elements and philosophy of nature, the extent and wonders of the universe, and the laws which govern the revolution of the countless millions of worlds that roll in immensity! What a difference in the degree of their religious culture, their knowledge of God and divine things, and their love of the pure and celestial, between a Channing and some ignorant, depraved wretch, thrown out upon society from some "Five Points'" den of infamy, and kicked and cursed through his existence on earth into his rude, pauper's grave! What a difference on their entrance into the future life, as to the development and growth of their intellects, between a Webster and some idiot. And yet, all these persons, and all others, will be *equally pure as to the substance and element of their being* and in the means of advancement in the divine and celestial in their new existence. In this respect they shall be "equal to the angels and are the children of God, *being* THE CHILDREN OF THE RESURRECTION."* No impartiality can enter Heaven. All, therefore, no matter what their profession or belief, must meet with a change, —a *radical* change, as we have seen,—before entering that sphere of purity and blessedness.

We know that the thought advanced here is not received with favor by many, especially by thousands of professed Christians. They are filled with disgust and offended pride at the thought of being placed on a level, even in this one particular, with the wretches we have described, on their entrance into the higher life. "Indeed," they say, in tones of scorn, "do you think *such* creatures are to be equally *pure* with *us* and mingle in *our* society in the heavenly world?" And why not, Christian

---
* Luke 20:36.

friends? Look into your own hearts, and notwithstanding your professions of goodness and purity, see the nest of vipers which sometimes rankle there, and which manifest themselves at times in your dislike and even hatred of others; your self-righteousness shown in these utterances; your disposition to malign, traduce and injure others; your ill-temper, your selfishness, your lusts and passions, your want of a forgiving spirit, your lack of gratitude to God! —Oh, think of all this, and ask yourself if you enter the Spirit World with this nature of sin still clinging to you, will *you* be fit for the purity of Heaven; and if the inhabitants of Heaven will not have reason to scorn and repudiate *you*, as you scorn and repudiate the wretches toward whom you exercise no charity and whom your pride and selfishness would exclude from Heaven if you had the power!

How can *you* have hope of becoming as the angels and *children of God*, only through the resurrection power of the Lord Jesus Christ, and the grace of that Being whose goodness is infinite? Surely this is all the hope *we* have; it is all you can have. And if you and the writer can be purified, thus washed and "made clean, through the blood of the Lamb," why not other sinners? And yet all this will not bring us upon the same plane of equality in the future life, as to our knowledge, our love of God, our moral and spiritual culture or in a thousand other respects. Probably the difference among men will be as great in the future world as it is in this. No two persons are precisely alike in this existence, either physically or intellectually. We do not *perfectly* resemble each other in *our persons*, or *our thoughts*, or *our feelings* in this life, though the *substance* and *essence* of our spiritual being may be similar. So in the future existence, men will probably differ as much in the particulars mentioned as in this, notwithstanding the essence and substance of their being will be similar.

2. Inasmuch as we shall enter upon the future life sinless in our nature, will that life be one of *progression*?

We answer, yes, thanks to God, it will! Not in the *purity of our existence*, however, but in knowledge, affection and in all that is divine and heavenly. What wonders and glories open up to our conception and imagination as we contemplate this great and blessed truth. Think of the conditions favorable to advancement into which mankind will be ushered in the resurrection existence. There we shall be divested of the hindrances and encumbrancs of this life, and by the perfection of our new, spiritual nature, we shall obtain knowledge, more as do the angels, by our intuitions. And this sublime privilege will be extended to the lowest and poorest and most depraved of this life as well as the most advanced. God is not partial when the whole of man's existence is considered. Though the soul, benighted by heathenism, never before knew God, it shall see Him as He is in the future life, and be attracted toward Him by the purity and glory of His character. Though it never before heard of His Son, the Teacher and Savior of the world, it shall now behold him in all the loveliness of his divine nature. Though it never before felt penitence for sin, gratitude to God for life, and the innumerable blessings of its existence, now this feeling will permeate its whole being, for it shall have knowledge of the grace and love and infinite goodness of our heavenly Father as displayed in all His works and all His providences. The truth and the purity of Heaven will attract us,—the immensity of the universe will fill us with delighted astonishment; the joy and spiritual beauty of the angels will win us, and our only desire and the chief source of our happiness will be to advance in the performance of new duties, to receive instruction from our divine Master and Savior, and to grow in grace and in a knowledge of God and His wonderful works and providences. Thus shall we ever progress; always reaching out our expanding energies toward the infinite, but never fully reaching or comprehending it.

3. And besides all this, the more we know of God and of our Savior, and the gifts and graces bestowed on us, the more gratitude we shall experience and the deeper will be our feeling of accountability to God. True, we shall have no desire or disposition to violate God's law. But to remain passive and indolent, though we commit no wrong, is not the duty nor the normal condition of intelligent beings,

even in this life. How then can it be in the next? There, we shall have employments. Heaven is not a place of idleness. Lounging and loafing and indolence, even though these be genteel, and are practiced in the homes of wealth, with servants to aid, never were a source of happiness in this world, and cannot constitute Heaven in the next. We must *do* something. "My Father hitherto worketh and I work," exclaimed the Master. The highest archangel, if the happiest of all the angels, it is because, being the most divine, he accomplishes more for himself and others, than all beside.

Yes we shall, we must *do* something in the future. This will be our divine aspiration. Our great gratitude to God, our deep obligations to Him, the example of the inhabitants of the celestial life, all will incite to deeds of duty under God, and to do His will. And this brings us to say,

4. That the more we accomplish in deeds of duty under God in that world, the greater our advancement in knowledge, and the more we shall progress in all that is divine and celestial, *the more of pure, unalloyed happiness we shall enjoy.* We do not believe there is anything like misery in the resurrection existence; and yet we do not believe that any two souls in that existence ever experience precisely the same amount of happiness. They do not here and they will not there. Every one will be happy, but only according to the advancement he has made in divine things as indicated in the foregoing.

And though in the future life some will be aware of the superior condition of others in consequence of superior knowledge and greater advancement in celestial life and duties, no discontent or jealousy or envy can be experienced in any soul in that pure and blessed life, for it will be one of universal love and good will. Each will have unfaltering trust in God and in the laws that govern his new, celestial existence. He will not have the capacity at once for affection so great as those more advanced, but his capacity, whatever it shall be, like cups of different capacity, all brimming with water, will be *full* of gratitude and love and pure and holy determinations, and he will be encouraged in the thought that by the law of progress which prevails, with proper patience, he shall at length reach higher realms and greater happiness.

These are briefly our thoughts concerning the subject under consideration. In Heaven all are clad in garments of celestial purity and glory; and yet there is infinite diversity there and perpetual and eternal progress, while our only desire will be to praise God by serving Him. Thanks to our Father in Heaven for these sublime and glorious truths! How do they thrill the soul with delight, especially as they enfold in their loving embrace the dear ones of its affection who have entered that world of angelic enjoyment, and are now sweeping forward in the realms of the true and celestial. And all shall arrive there at last. No father or mother, parent or child, brother or sister shall be absent, for the promise of the blessed Savior is, "I, if I be lifted up from the earth, will draw ALL men unto me!"

"Come to me thoughts of Heaven!
My happy spirit bear
On your bright wings, by morning giv'n,
Up to celestial air!
Away, far, far away
From thoughts by passion giv'n,
Fold me in pure, still, cloudless day,
O, blessed thoughts of Heaven!

"Come in my chasten'd hour,
Sweet thoughts! and yet again
O'er sinful wish and mem'ry show'r
Your soft, effacing rain;
Waft me where gales divine
With dark clouds ne'er have striven,
Where living founts forever thine;
O, blessed thoughts of Heav'n!

CHAPTER XIX.

Rewards and Punishments---Will they be Meted out in the Resurrection Life?

Why Punish a Being who is Pure and Holy and can never more Commit a Wrong?—The Doctrine of the Church not believed by the Church. —The Doctrine of Rewards —The Scriptures silent on the Subject.— What is Punishment?—It is Corrective and hence cannot be Endless.

THE above is a question of great interest and importance. It is often asked by both the old and young. Even clergymen of our own sect, as may be seen by the first of these chapters, are not always fully determined in their own minds concerning it. It is a question, moreover, intimately related to the general subject embraced in this volume, and directly involved in it. To consider it as fully as our limits will permit will be the object of this chapter.

Of course, the reader who has felt interest sufficient to follow our course of reasoning in what we have thus far written, in this volume, has formed an opinion which may be pretty correct relative to what our conclusions *must* be, as drawn from the premises which we think we have already legitimately established, viz., that in the other life men shall possess sinless natures; natures only to love God and goodness, and to be influenced by the spiritual and divine;—natures that shall never more know sin but only be influenced by upward attractions and tendencies forever and ever.

Now why *punish* any being who will never more commit a wrong? We can believe in punishment for sin in the resurrection life only on the basis that men will sin in that life. But how can they sin unless they possess natures that will incite them to sin; that is, sinful natures? And if they possess sinful natures *on their entrance* into the other life, will they not *always* possess sinful natures? Can the Ethiopian change his skin or the leopard his spots? Can men work any radical change in their natures? And if they possess sinful natures in that life will they not sin always, and hence suffer punishment for sin always? It looks so to us, and hence this kind of Gospel, entertained by some of the professedly educated among us, is not Gospel, but the doctrine of endless sinning and endless suffering as advocated in these latter times, by all the leading minds of the so-called evangelical sects. For the doctrine propagated by these sects to-day is, not that men shall be punished endlessly for the sins of this brief life,—as this, they admit, would be an outrage upon all justice,—but that men who die with hearts unregenerated will carry with them into the other world this condition of soul, and as there can be no change for the better in that other life, they will continue to sin endlessly and hence will suffer endlessly the consequences of their sins. This, we admit, is more reasonable than the old idea that God would visit one trifling sin committed in this life with unmitigated and endless pain. But it is still the doctrine of endless sin and endless punishment, is positively contradicted by the New Testament, and hence should be positively rejected by the Christian.

But it is proper that we state our views on the subject under consideration, more at length and more clearly than these thoughts suggest;—and we remark,

1. That the doctrine of future rewards and punishments has long been a doctrine of the church. It is the doctrine in which we were educated in childhood and youth. It is what we believed before we arrived at maturity. We were not taught in *present* rewards and punishments, but were instructed by the preaching we heard and the books we read, that if we lived a life of purity and virtue in this world, though we must surrender many of the pleasurable enjoyments of the irreligious in this life, we should surely be rewarded *in the world to come*, for all our faithfulness. On the contrary, if we lived a life of disobedience toward God, though we might enjoy more in this world than the devoted Christian, *in the world to come* we should surely be punished and punished endlessly for all our transgressions.

So said all the clergy whom we heard preach when a youth, and so *professed* to believe all the good Christian people with whom we had intercourse. And yet, *really* not one of them believed a word of what they professed, for they propagated, right upon the top of this, the doctrine that in Heaven, the receptacle of Christians, there was experienced only unspeakable enjoyment. Many who enter there, it was admitted, were very wicked a portion of their lives in this world. But if they only enjoy the delights and glories of Heaven in the other world, how are they punished there for the evil deeds of this life? And then again in the hell of the other life, men are only tortured, endlessly, irretrievably tortured. They are *rewarded* for nothing good done in this life; and yet many of them were marvels of goodness while in this world. We once heard a preacher affirm in the pulpit, that Benjamin Franklin was suffering the pains of the damned; and so was Thomas Jefferson and Tom Paine, because they "*died impenitent.*" But these men were all kind men, benevolent men, who, by their excellent works, blest many souls in this life. And yet as they only suffer in the world to come, how can they be *rewarded* for the good deeds of this world?

But though we assented to these views of future rewards and punishments, at that early time of life, we have no sympathy for them at the present time for several reasons; one is, because the Bible does not teach them. It is all essential that the Christian should base his faith on the word of inspiration; but one will search in vain in the Bible, for the doctrine of rewards in the resurrection existence for the acts of a righteous life, or for punishment in that state for the evil deeds of this world.

The sum of all that is revealed in the Bible of man's future being, as we have abundantly shown in these chapters, is that that life is a spiritual, heavenly, angelic, immortal, incorruptible, glorious existence, where sin, death, decay, pain and sorrow can never more touch and torture us, as in this world, but where there is one onward, upward sweep of the soul in its approximation toward God, in knowledge and truth, and divine aspirations and happiness, forever and forever, but never reaching him! This is the condition in which the New Testament reveals man in the resurrection life,—and in this condition it LEAVES HIM. It describes not in what section of God's vast universe Heaven is, nor what employments shall engage its inhabitants, nor in what way, if any, they will be effected by the experiences of this life, and the nature that they here possess. Neither Christ, nor Paul, nor any other of the apostles, deemed it necessary to open up to the consciousness of the soul, facts touching these questions, but instead have only given us statements of great truths as the basis of a hope, "sure and steadfast as an anchor to the soul," that we are bound to a purer and better world than this; are heirs of an "inheritance incorruptible, undefiled, and that faded not away," and that though the nature of all its enjoyments in that life is not described, enough is said to impart the assurance that they are too high for our comprehension,—indeed, are among the things that are "unutterable" by mortal tongue, for "eye hath not seen, nor ear heard, neither can the mind conceive" the excellency of its glory.

By all this it will be seen that the Bible is utterly silent as to the subject in question, and if any man professes to *know* that God will bring men to awful judgments in the future life, to be followed by punishments for the sins of this world, he is wise above the divine oracles, for they say nothing about it.

To be sure men have their convictions on this subject. We have ours; but these convictions are not so much authorized by the teachings of the Scriptures, as they are a deduction from reason and the nature of things as they exist. We believe that men suffer loss in this life by their disobedience and folly, and will enter Heaven with a knowledge of this fact in their minds. And, notwithstanding the great change that will be wrought in their constitutional nature by a change of worlds, they will not occupy so exalted a place in the galaxy of spiritual intelligence and spiritual happiness, as those who have made the most of their present existence by striving for heavenly wisdom, for a love of benevolence, for activity in a life of humanity, and cultivating a desire for perfection in all things divine. Here is loss. Every soul must realize its condition in the resurrection life when compared with that of other souls. And thus will be felt in the other world, the character and circumstances of our lives in this world;—our providential advantages or disadvantages from which spring our knowledge or ignorance; our growth spiritually or our imbecility, our virtues or our vices in this life. Some regard these different conditions of gain on the one part, and loss on the other, in the light of *rewards* and *punishments;* but we look upon them as legitimate but varied consequences springing from the different providences that accompany men in the circumstances of their birth, life, education and all that belongs to their experiences in the present world. The inequalities of another life, to which we have referred, can exist, even though men are justly rewarded and punished in this life for the deeds of this life, and, notwithstanding the future existence, is, as the New Testament reveals it, incorruptible, heavenly, spiritual, glorious, immortal, and hence a world of enjoyment to all who enter there.

With these thoughts in mind, let us consider more at length the true, Scriptural doctrine of rewards and punishments. We repeat, one may search in vain in the Bible for the doctrine of rewards in the resurrection existence for the acts of a righteous life; or for punishment in that state for the evil deeds of this world. And yet no doctrine is plainer or more positively taught in the Bible than that of rewards and punishments.

What is *reward?* It is *recompense—compensation—something paid.*

The common idea taught by the church is, that in the future world, God will *compensate* us for keeping his commandments in this life. Heaven will be given as a "*reward* for good deeds." But, we repeat, the Bible teaches no such doctrine. Its language; on the contrary, is, "*In* keeping the commandments there *is* great reward." That is, the *act* of obedience to the divine law contains its own reward. David assures us that "great peace *have* they that love God's law." Every true Christian understands the meaning of these declarations. He has the testimony within himself that every day devoted to the spirit and principles of the religion of Christ, carries with it its own compensation. He feels that "the kingdom of Heaven *is* righteousness, peace and joy in the Holy Ghost," and that "it is *within* him." That "the reward of humility *is* riches and honor and life," as the wise man declares. That if a man comes to God daily in prayer, like David of old, he will "*find* Him," and "*be delivered*" from his troubles, and "strengthened with strength" in his soul. That if he have faith, he shall experience the truth of the divine promise, through the prophet, "Thou wilt keep him *in perfect peace* whose mind is stayed on thee, *because he trusteth in thee ;*" and of the declaration of another prophet, "Blessed *is* the man that trusteth in the Lord;" and of the apostle Paul, "We that have believed do *enter into rest.*" The very object of religion is to make us happy, hopeful, blessed, *while we live.* If a man loves God supremely and his neighbor as himself, what happiness he experiences *from this very condition of soul!* And having thus lived all his life, in the enjoyment of peace and trust and spiritual blessedness, shall he demand future eternal happiness as *compensation* for the little good he has accomplished in this world? How unreasonable! The true Christian will not ask it; he *does* not! It is true, he anticipates a world of glory when God calls him to His sweet and blessed Home in Heaven, not as a *reward*, not as *wages* however, but as the free gift of God's great love, "through the Lord and Savior Jesus Christ."

Such is the Scriptural doctrine of *rewards.* Let us now turn to the subject of *punishment.*

What is the Scriptural doctrine of punishment? What is the *object* of the divine law, and of the *penalty* attached to that law?

The mass of Christians have long entertained the idea that God's law is simply an expression of his arbitrary will, without regard to the present good or happiness of His creatures;—that the penalty attached is future, endless pain, and that, hence, the idea of *reformation, improvement, obedience* and the enjoyment which these secure as the *object* and *end* of punishment, are no part of the divine plan. It is believed by many that God treats His children as the State treats a criminal. A man murders his fellow in this or some other State. The "strong arm of the law" seizes him, brings him to the bar of judgment, condemns him and throws him into prison, there to toil and suffer during his natural life; or it orders that he be taken from his cell, after the lapse of a given time, and hanged upon a gibbet until he is dead. The idea of making him better, of instructing, elevating and blessing him, *in* the infliction of the pain it produces, is never considered by the State. It is not the *object* of State penalties. Why not? Because the laws of the State are but a reflex of the laws of God as comprehended by our fathers who enacted them. This is the rule that controls the Almighty in his punishment of the offender, as they believed, and as the large majority of Christians still believe. God has given man His law, they say. The present existence is a world of probation. Those who violate said law and die with their sins unrepented of, God will bring to His bar in the immortal world, condemn them and consign them to the prison-house of hell, from which there can be *no release and no end.*

And this is punishment as inflicted by God. So says the church, and hence it is made the ground of punishment as inflicted by the State. We trust the time is coming when the State will act from higher, purer and diviner motives. But we do not expect it till the Christian world is redeemed from the great error which lies at the basis of all its inhumanity and wrong as connected with the subject now under consideration.

The question returns: What is the *Scriptural doctrine of punishment?* What is the *object* of the divine law and of the *penalty* attached to that law?

The object of God's law is the proper government of His rational creatures—His children—that they may enjoy all it is possible for human beings to enjoy while on earth. God is good—*infinitely* good. He is our kind, loving Father, who desires our happiness while we live in the present world, and has promised us future endless blessedness as the free gift of His infinite love. If we violate His laws we *suffer*; but the design of this very suffering is to *correct* us, *improve* us, and bring us back to Him. See how plain the teachings of the inspired Word, on this subject:—

"Behold *happy* is the man whom God *correcteth;* therefore despise not thou the chastening of the Almighty; for He maketh sore and He bindeth up; He woundeth and His hands make whole." So the wise man says: "It is good for me that I have been afflicted, for before I was afflicted I went astray, but now have I kept thy word." "My son, despise not thou the *chastening* of the Lord, nor weary of His *correction;* for whom the Lord loveth He *correcteth,* even as a Father the son in whom he delighteth." Here the chastisements of God are compared to those of a loving, earthly parent, who corrects his child for the child's good; because he loves him and "delighteth" in him. The same idea is repeated and emphasized by Paul in his letter to the Hebrews: "My son, despise not thou the chastening of the Lord, nor faint when thou art rebuked of Him. For whom the Lord loveth He chasteneth, and scourgeth every son whom He receiveth. * * Furthermore, we have had fathers of our flesh which corrected us, and we gave them reverence; shall we not much rather be in subjection unto the Father of spirits and live? For *they* verily for a few days chastened us after their own pleasure; but *He* for our profit, that we might be partakers of His holiness. Now, no chastening for the present seemeth joyous but grievous; nevertheless it *afterward yieldeth the peaceable fruit of righteousness unto them which are exercised thereby.*"

We connot withhold the remarks of an eminent Biblical scholar, on this language, they are so in harmony with our own views, notwithstanding he was a Methodist divine. He says: "All this is proof of the fatherly love of God Almighty. Our natural parents were *correctors*, and we reverenced *them* notwithstanding their corrections often arose from *whim* or *caprice*. Shall we not rather be in subjection to the Father of our spirits, to Him from whom we have received both body and soul; who is our *Creator, Preserver* and *Supporter;* to whom both we and our parents owe our life, our blessings, our all, and who corrects us only '*for our profit, that we may be partakers of His holiness;*' and though for the present it often seemeth *grievous*, yet it afterward '*yieldeth* the peaceable fruits of righteousness unto those who are exercised thereby.'"

All this is well. To it we can respond a hearty amen! But then how could this honored divine, or any other man, reconcile these declarations with the doctrine that millions upon millions of the human race will be visited by this same Almighty God with *endless* pains in the world of woe for the sins of this life? Is there any afterward to *endless* wretchedness? And does that ever "yield the peaceable fruits of righteousness to those who are exercised" by it?

From all this it will be seen that all true punishment is *corrective.* This is its object. Hence it is impossible for men to sin and not feel the consequences of their wickedness. "*In the day thou eatest thereof,* thou shalt surely die." "The way of the transgressor *is* hard and there *is* no peace for the wicked, saith my God." The *object* of the unhappy condition of mind described here, is to influence the sinner to forsake his sins and turn to God in righteousness. "*Thine own wickedness shall correct thee,* and thy backslidings shall reform thee; know therefore and see, that it *is* an evil thing and bitter that thou hast forsaken the Lord thy God." Here is described by the prophet the bitterness of sin; and not only so, but the declaration is plainly given that this bitterness was *designed* to *correct* and *would* correct, those who should walk in its paths. This, we repeat, is punishment. (*Kolasis*). It is the infliction of pain in consequence of a neglect, or violation of duty, *with a view to correct the evil.** Every *good* earthly parent acts on this principle in punishing his children. He visits them *with pain* with a view to *correct them*, and prevent their repeating the offensive or injurious act. Are you a father or mother and do you ever strike your child or in any manner chastise it, simply to graitfy your malignant feelings? If so, you are in the wrong. This is *vengeance* and not *punishment* as the latter always demands the good, improvement, elevation and blessing of the soul visited with its stripes.

Again: Your child has violated your law. You are about to visit him with pain. Now were you *perfectly certain* that he would never again commit a similar offense, would there exist *any necessity* for the infliction of the threatened chastisement? Nay, we go further and ask, if you possessed *absolute knowledge* that such would be the condition of your child in his disposition, desires and power to resist temptation from this time forward, as that he would never more violate your commands, and you should torture him with pain *because of his past acts*, would *you* not be guilty of wrong and yourself be deserving of chastisement? This is our view of the

---
* Smith on Divine Government.

case. No matter what *your* child has done—nor what any child of God has done, if, through repentture or regeneration, or *any* change in his moral naance or constitution we could absolutely know that he would never again do wrong, it would be utterly unnecessary, and only the spirit of malignancy that could torture him because of what he had done. Nowhere can it be shown that this is *God's rule*. Nowhere in all the Bible, can this idea be found as connected with God's dealings with His creatures in this life. And hence we cannot believe it will be the rule with Him in His dealings with His children in the future, resurrection life. We have shown in these chapters, plainly enough we think, that such will be the constitutional nature of man in the world to come that he will no longer be tempted to sin, or possess a disposition or inclination to violate, in any sense, the laws of his Creator. He will no longer be incited to murder, or rob, or utter falsehoods, or be guilty of drunkenness, or moved with envy, passion or hatred, as in this life. And hence to visit him in the future with pain because of the errors and evils of this existence, would not only be an act for which there could exist no necessity, but it must be the offspring of retaliation or revenge, a feeling which we do not believe it possible for a God of infinite goodness and purity to possess.

These are our views of this subject. Show us that we shall still possess sinful natures in the resurrection life and transgress the laws of God there as here, and we will admit that we shall be visited with punishment in that existence. But the divine Word positively declares that "the righteous *shall be* recompensed IN THE EARTH, *much more* the wicked and the sinner." This declaration is plain; so plain that there is no mistaking its meaning. If, then, both the "righteous" and the "wicked" are "recompensed" or "rewarded" "*in the earth*," for the deeds done in the earth, and the Bible nowhere inculcates the idea that they are "recompensed" in eternity, why should we not confide in God's word? Why should we contend for the truth of that which God Himself declares to be false; which our reason and all our instincts condemn and which we desire should be false? Show us that the Bible when properly understood, contains the doctrine of future rewards and punishments, as the inculcation of our Father in Heaven, and we will admit its correctness. But, until this is done, we must cherish the sweet convictions, which, years ago, were instrumental in up-rooting in our youthful soul the old errors of *endless* punishment, and which are only strengthened more and more by reflection and investigation.

"There is no sorrow, friends, but it has still
Some soul of sweetness in it; there's no ill
But comes from Him who made it, and is good
As fruit in season, leaf in budding wood."

CHAPTER XX.

Partial Evil and Inequality Harmonized with Infinite Goodness.

Inequalities of this World.—No two are precisely the same at Death.—How can they occupy precisely the same Conditions in the Resurrection?—Impossible to Harmonize an Endless Evil with Infinite Goodness.—Man is Imperfect but not placed wrong.—God makes no Mistakes.—Each one in the Future shall be Perfectly Happy in His Sphere.

WE have presented it as our *belief* in these pages that the resurrection life is no more a condition of *equality* for the millions of happy spirits who people the world of glory, than this existence. As it regards degrees of knowledge, or divine aspiration, or divine love, or as to degree of enjoyment we shall possess, when considered in the light of *comparison*, the same difference and diversity will exist in the other life, that we find in this world. As we have before stated, this belief is not based on any distinct and positive declaration of the Bible, for the Bible is silent on the subject, but is a deduction from reason and what it seems to us must be a necessary consequence of things as they exist.

One dies an infant, another in the full strength of developed manhood, another an idiot, another a Newton, another with his religious feelings and sentiments dwarfed, another a Fenelon or Channing, another after a life of sinful indulgence, another after a life of holiness. In the future, though raised in incorruption, spirituality, power and glory, we cannot conceive, as we have before said, though sinless in their nature, how they can occupy precisely the same condition, or stand on a perfect equality as it regards the degree of intelligence they will possess, the strength of their aspirations for divine things, or even in degree of happiness.

Others have their views on this subject, we suppose. These are ours. We have long entertained them and the more we investigate the subject, and reflect upon it, the stronger are our convictions of their correctness. We offer them in this place because they legitimately come into this discussion, and because many who have written us with inquiries cannot harmonize them with the *infinite* and *impartial* goodness of God. They ask "if God is *impartially* and *infinitely* good, how can he be the author of an existence of inequality for men?" They think if he possesses this character, he is a being of absolute *injustice* and *must lack* in the element of either goodness, wisdom or power. "If he were infinitely and impartially good and wise and powerful, there could be none of this inequality in the future." So they argue.

But we do not so regard the subject. We are aware that to reconcile the existence of an *infinite* or *endless* evil,—such as is enforced by the creeds of the self-styled evangelical sects,—in their doctrine of *endless* punishment for the soul, with the idea of infinite goodness is an impossibility; but not *partial* or *transient* evil, or evil which shall be so controlled as to *result in* the greater good of those who are exercised by it. We believe there is truth in the declaration of the poet :—

> "All nature is but art unknown to thee;
> All chance, direction, which thou canst not see;
> All partial evil, universal good,
> All discord, harmony, not understood."

God's goodness is "infinite" and "impartial." We believe this with an unfaltering trust, and yet we behold not only a conditon of inequality among men in the present world as the fruit of God's creative power, but we behold men in a condition of sin and suffering in this life. Entirely of His own will, and by His own sovereign power, without consulting the desire of any creature in the universe, God has brought into being millions upon millions of human, sentient beings, and so directed the circumstances of their birth and lives, as that much of this very existence of *some* of them is a curse to them, while others are so favored by the providence which surrounds them in birth, wealth, religious privileges and education, that their existence in this life, is much more favorable, and a source of far greater enjoyment. We are now speaking of extreme cases, where there can be no question relative to the disparity in condition and happiness between persons, and not of the masses, the aggregate of whose happiness is very similar.

Now "why this disparity or inequality?" Persons ask this question in their ignorance and their circumscribed faith, and never with the thought of man's entire existence in *time and eternity*, and the necessity of his occupying the imperfect condition of a human being before he rises to the angelic and sweeps upward and onward in his sphere of holiness and progression toward the infinite and eternal!

> "Of systems possible, if 'tis confessed,
> That wisdom infinite must form the best,
> Where all must fall, or not coherent be,
> And all that rises, rise in due degree,
> Then in the scale of reasoning life, 'tis plain
> There must be somewhere, such a rank as man.
> And all the question (wrangle e'er so long)
> Is only this, if God has placed him wrong."

We do not believe He has placed him "wrong," for man is the result not only of infinite "wisdom" but of "infinite *goodness*." Human beings are what God designed them to be,—men and women,—with the powers, capacities and imperfections of men and women; and though God, in the creation of man, was moved by the impulse of infinite and impartial goodness, all are subjects of sin in this life, while no two on earth are precisely similar in person, or mind, or heart, nor is the *condition* of any two precisely alike. How wonderful this dissimilarity! And shall we say that God is not good, or that he is partial because of this dissimilarity, or of man's imperfect, sinful condition in this life? Have we no faith in God's goodness, or that He will act from the impulse of His divine love in extricating man from this condition of imperfection and partial unhappiness? Any *man* whose heart is filled with sympathy for his race, would do this if he had the power; and shall we doubt Him whose goodness is infinite and therefore is more than sufficient for the sins and imperfections of the whole human race? How do these sins loom up before us, rising like mountains in awful grandeur toward the throne of God! All men are buried beneath them. From whence shall they find deliverance? God's goodness, gushing out toward His great family, which He is "bringing in a way they know not," answers the question. "Behold the Lamb of God that TAKETH AWAY THE SIN OF THE WORLD!" "Where sin abounded, GRACE did MUCH-MORE ABOUND!" "So that as sin hath reigned unto death, even so might grace reign through righteousness UNTO ETERNAL LIFE by Jesus Christ the Lord!" Blessed declaration!

Here is the condition of the great family of man in the life to come, and all is to be experienced and enjoyed in consequence of God's impartial love for men. The "sin of the world" is removed. "Death and him that hath the power of death—that is, the devil"—are destroyed, and "love," and "life," and "incorruptibility," and "glory," and "immortality," only shall be known forever and ever, by the great family over whom God is Father and Friend! In view of this glorious consummation, can we not exclaim in the language of an eminent evangelical commentator, when reflecting upon the same enrapturing theme:—"Here is glory to him that loved us, and washed us from our sins in his own blood, and has made us kings and priests unto God, and his Father, to whom be glory and dominion forever and ever, amen! Hallelujah! The Lord God omnipotent reigneth! Amen! and amen!"

Now when the human family shall have been brought into this exalted condition of purity, happiness and glory, "death having been swallowed up *in victory ;*"—when they shall behold the goodness and wisdom of God in all the providences of their existence, and shall see that after all, the seeming partialities of this life were not partialities, but providences tending to the good of all, will any murmur or find cause for complaint? Will not their souls rather be filled with love and gratitude and praise to God for His great goodness and His loving kindness to the children of men?

To our comprehension, all this is reasonable and perfectly in harmony with the infinite wisdom and impartial goodness of God.

"And so it is to my comprehension thus far," says the objector, "but how about the inequalities in the life to come described in these chapters? Can they be harmonized with the wisdom and goodness of God?"

We answer, perfectly, as we view the subject, because that life is no longer a condition of sin, or servitude, or darkness, or of suffering in any sense, but only one of light and love, and purity, and spirituality, and glory, and progression, and peace. No positive unhappiness can be known in Heaven. All will enjoy there, and their enjoyment will be *full*, and yet it must be graduated by the capacity of each for enjoyment. The little child, in this life, is delighted with a rattle and its enjoyment is full. The more matured, with a larger capacity, demand something more substantial to fill them with happiness. Both are *filled;* hence no partiality is discovered. Here are a father and mother in this life, with several children of all ages from infancy to maturity, who constitute their family. Suppose that by some fatal, contagious disease, they all pass suddenly to the higher and diviner life. How are they advanced spiritually and in their capacity for love, and knowledge, and enjoyment, by the developments of the resurrection! They loved each other in this life, but how much purer and more intense their affection now. How are their souls lifted up, and what rapture and what praise to God do they experience in this new existence so divine and glorious! The enjoyment of each soul is full, and yet the enjoyments of no two are precisely *equal*. Their intellectual capacities are wonderfully quickened, and their ability to grasp knowledge, or to know intuitively, enhanced, and to such an extent, that no human being in his earth life, can either vie with them or even conceive of the wonderful change which is thus wrought—and yet, diversity of intellect and degrees of knowledge exist there as here. But in all this we discover no partiality of love. Nor will any such feeling be experienced or be possible in the other existence, as pride or jealousy or the thought that God has exalted one above another, because all will there have been "born of God" and will "know" Him and love Him with their whole might and strength and their neighbors as themselves. Their penitence for the sins of this world will be sincere and complete. Seeing God in all the purity and beauty of His nature, the soul will be attracted to Him by a law as natural as that which turns the needle to the pole. The divine Word declares the existence of an "innumerable company of angels," and "legions of angels," and speaks of the "mighty angels," and the "high archangels;" and we believe that in the realms of God's universe, there are millions upon millions, and billions of happy, spiritual intelligencies, whose aspirations and desires are all in harmony with the divine will, and whose knowledge is far above that of any inhabitant of earth. We cannot conceive that all these glorious beings, though they are all sinless and happy in their sphere, stand on a perfect level as to intelligence, spiritual aspirations and spiritual enjoyment, for they are not so represented. Rather do we believe that there is a scale of being at the top of which is the Almighty Himself, the Great First Cause of all. Between Him and the highest created intelligences, an infinite distance must exist; but from the highest order of created intelligence, it appears to us there must be gradation, or at least variety—to the lowest, so to speak;—all angelic, intelligent and happy according to their several powers and capacities, as represented by Paul in the 15th chapter of his letter to the Corinthians. He says:—"There is one glory of the sun, and another glory of the moon, and another glory of the stars; for one star differeth from another star in glory;" so also, is the "resurrection from the dead," or those who are resurrected; that is, they are *all* stars, all glorious, all effulgent, but they "differ" in their effulgence or glory. They are not all precisely similar, though they are all divine, spiritual, happy; for he goes on to declare, as we have before seen, that they are raised in "incorruption," "glory" and power" and with spiritual bodies, and as Christ declares, are "equal to the angels of God in Heaven, being the children of the resurrection."

How beautiful is this conception and how exalted and grand the subject. In view of it, and the diversity and inequality which it presents, where do we behold partiality or lack of wisdom in our dear, loving Father in Heaven, God over all blessed forevermore? If these views will not fill the soul with unfaltering trust in Him, we know not what will.

CHAPTER XXI.

Shall We Know Each Other in Heaven?

Those who have passed into the Higher Life can see us and they know us.—This is not the Hope of all.—Reasons for Belief in this Beautiful Truth.—If we have no knowledge of our Friends in Heaven, we shall have no knowledge of anything that existed on Earth.—Teachings of the Bible relative to the Subject.—Thoughts Sublimely Beautiful.

TO us the above is a question full of interest. We always think of the dear ones gone as still living very near to us. If they are not so personally, they are in their sympathies and affections. Though we think of them as being in Heaven,—a place of wonderful perfection and glory, and at a distance from our earth,—still we cannot help feeling that so wonderfully improved are all their senses and intuitions, that they see us, and know constantly of our condition, and are round and about us somewhat in the sense that God is round about us, and that when our heavenly Father sees fit to call us to the diviner life, those nearest to us in their sympathies and affections, will be nearest to us to welcome us with sweetest smiles and celestial joy, as we pass out of the earthly into the heavenly.

Of course, all this is based upon the certainty of

the fact that we shall know them, and they us, on our entrance into the other life. They know us *now* as we exist in our earthly homes;—why will they not continue to know us, and why shall we not know them in our exalted, heavenly Home? If no such knowledge will really exist on our entrance into that more celestial world, then all our sweetest expectations and delightful anticipations, growing out of this sublime and comforting faith, will prove abortive. Hence, we repeat, this question is one of great interest to us.

But not so with all. Indeed, with many, the subject of a future existence has no special interest. They are in the prime of life and vigor of health. They have never been bereft. No cry of sorrow comes to them from the tomb. No dark pall rests upon their homes or their hearts. The dear ones God has given them are still with them. They are the light and joy of their earthly homes. They mingle in daily or weekly or yearly communion. They constitute the same unbroken circle. Father, mother, husband, wife, children, brothers, sisters are all *here*. Why should they think of their home in Heaven, or ask, "Will the dear ones know me? Shall I know them, and press them to my heart in ecstasy of joy when I reach the diviner life?"

But to those of us who have suffered bereavements;—whose family circles have been broken by the hand of death, and those as dear to us as our own existence have been removed forever from our earthly homes,—how different our thoughts, our feelings, our aspirations! Now we think of Heaven and the dear ones there. Heaven has a name and a place with us, for it is the home of those we love. It shall be *our* home by and by, and the home of all God's great family. And every question that refers to it, or to those whom it contains, or to us in connection with it and them, is full of interest.

And to us, next to the happiness of those who have departed for the better life, there is no thought more comforting and blessed than that they have knowledge of those who are left. That whether we are weighed down by bereavement, or exist in poverty, or are staggering under the burdens of sin and sorrow, or are in the enjoyment of health and happiness,—those in Heaven we love, and who love us, know of our condition, and sympathize with it, and that when we have done with earth and all its affairs, we shall enter into the enjoyment of their spiritual presence, identify them, have knowledge of what interests them, and associate and commune with them in a manner more tender, and in sweeter and diviner union, than ever before. All this we believe to be true. And from our experience in the sick room, around the bed of the dying, and when called to administer consolation in the house of sorrow, we know how very dear is this faith, and this thought to those of whom we speak.

In giving expression to a few considerations designed to strengthen the faith of all into whose hands these pages may fall, in the truth of this comforting thought, we would say,

1. That if what we have described above is *not* true,—that is, if in Heaven we shall have no knowledge of our friends there, so as to recognize them,— then we shall have no knowledge that they exist before they enter Heaven,—or while they live on earth. Indeed, we shall have no knowledge of anybody or anything that existed on earth. For if, in changing worlds, we shall lose all recollection and all knowledge of our nearest relatives, father or mother, husband or wife, or child,—so as not to be able to know them in the other life,—how is it possible we shall have recollection of anything that existed on earth? If the mother will have no knowledge of her own child in Heaven, "flesh of her flesh and bone of her bone," so as to identify him,—then what will she know that existed in the earth? Indeed, how will she know that there was such a place as this earth and that she had being here prior to her existence in the spirit world? And if all this is true, what is death but annihilation? Annihilation of all memory of the past; all knowledge of anything and everything that transpired or existed, and all affection for those we love. And what is another life, but another existence which begins where this ends? On this hypothesis we shall have memory in Heaven, but, like the memory of this life, it will reach

no further back than the commencement of our existence in that new state of being.

Our thoughts and knowledge and affections will have no concern with a prior existence. Indeed, we shall be just as ignorant of a prior existence as we are now ignorant of any existence which it is possible we may have enjoyed or suffered previous to the present life.

Moreover, to say that we shall have being in another state, with no knowledge of the past, is but to promise what the Atheist believes, and for which the Darwinians contend,—simply a succession of other beings when the present is no more. If, when our bodies die, all thought and memory die with them, so that when we enter another state or condition, we cannot *identify ourselves*, then will our future being be a *new creation*. It will not be *we* who will exist in that diviner life, but other beings created from us. And here we are brought to remark,

2. That this idea utterly repudiates and annihilates the plain Christian doctrine of the resurrection. The life from the dead which is everywhere promised in the Gospel, is *our* life and that of those dear to us,—all our fellow creatures indeed,—so that we should be comforted concerning our friends who are fallen asleep, through the blessed hope that they shall live with us and we with them in a sweet and blessed immortality,—a holy and blissful communion. The promise of the dear Master to Martha and Mary, in the moment of their great grief, was,

"*Thy brother* shall rise again;" meaning that *he* should live again; not that some other being should be created from their brother, and live again. And, his declaration to the thief, was,—"To-day, shalt *thou* be with me in Paradise;"—not that another being, having no identity with his former self, should be with him in the spirit world.

From all this, how plain it is that the scriptural doctrine of the resurrection promises our being a future life in such a manner as unmistakably to insure our identity, and that of those we love, in the blessed world to which we go? But,

3. Some say that the Scriptures are utterly silent on this interesting subject; that they nowhere affirm that the inhabitants of this world will know and recognize each other in the other life, notwithstanding they plainly declare the resurrection of all men into another existence. If this is true,—which we do not admit,—it is for the most natural reason imaginable. If another existence, far more exalted and beatific than this, is promised man as an antidote for death, his identity is inevitably involved in the fact and the hope of that other existence; and to assure him that he will recognize those he loves in that other life, would be quite as superfluous as would be the assurance to a circle of intimate friends, who, to rid themselves of our cold climate, are about to visit the sunny climes of Italy, that when they arrive in that land of fragrance and flowers they will still know each other,—for this is

what they positively anticipate. Indeed, they dream of nothing else. So it was with Christ and the loving disciples of our Lord. His promise was, "In my Father's House are many mansions. * * I go to prepare a place for you, and if I go and prepare a place for you I will come again and receive you unto myself, that where *I* am there *ye* may be also." Christ did not add :—"And ye shall know me and recognize each other, in those celestial mansions,"—for this was precisely what they would anticipate. To be with Christ in Heaven, and have no knowledge of the fact that it was Christ, would preclude the possibility of a knowledge that he was their Savior, or that they once had existence in a sinful world.

Again, as we have seen, the promise of Christ to the thief upon the cross was, "To-day shalt thou be with me in Paradise!" But Christ made no further declaration to the effect that having arrived in Paradise they would know each other. This would have been superfluous, as spiritual presence insured the certainty of spiritual recognition; and it was on the fact of recognition, and a knowledge of the spiritual presence of Christ, that was based the blessing of the promise.

Again, Paul and Peter and John and Stephen all expected to be exalted to glory and meet each other and their dear Lord in the world of bliss. And the bright expectation of a realization of this blessed thought filled them with joy "unspeakable and full of glory," causing them to shout "Thanks be to God, which giveth us the victory through our Lord and Savior Jesus Christ." But what "victory" could the resurrection prove to them unless their identity in the future life was *certain?* This was the very thing they anticipated. Their bodies would pass through the change called death, but *they* would still live in the "building of God, the house not made with hands, eternal in the heavens;" and though they had no positive promise of a knowledge of Christ and of each other in the divine life, this comforting thought is involved in the very idea of another existence, and was the chief source of all their joy. Indeed, it is the chief source of the Christian's joy to-day, as he anticipates meeting those he loves in the world of glory. To assure him that he and the dear objects of his affection will live again, but in ignorance of each other,—wandering through the realms of the celestial Eden for ages in search of those so precious, but never finding them, because of their inability to recognize them,—would deprive the soul of all its bliss, and fill Heaven with sobbing and tears.

From all this it will be seen that the recognition of our friends in Heaven is fully taught, at least by inference, in the Scriptures of the New Testament, to which we have referred. But beyond this, we come now to state,

4. That to our apprehension, this doctrine is plainly and positively declared by the apostle Paul

in the 13th chapter of his letter to the Corinthian Church, where, in contrasting the knowledge of the present with that of our future life, he employs the following plain words :—

"For we know in part, and we prophesy in part, but when that which is perfect is come, then that which is in part shall be done away. * * For now we see through a glass darkly, but then face to face; now I know in part; but then I shall know even as also I am known."

The meaning of these wondrous words is very cheering and very hopeful. In this world, the knowledge of men is exceedingly circumscribed. We know only "in part;" a very minute fraction, indeed, of what is to be known in the universe of God. All human knowledge is imperfect. Hence, our many mistakes and errors and sins. "But when that which is perfect is come,"—in other words, when we shall have entered on our life of heavenly perfection, where God's own light shall illumine the soul, and enable it to comprehend all truth with which it shall come in contact,—"then that which is in part shall be done away;" that is, the partial glimpses of knowledge we now attain to, shall cease, just as the stars fade out in the full glare of the meridian sun. Not that man will possess all knowledge on his entrance into Heaven, for omniscience alone belongs to the Almighty; but only that his soul will be no longer enshrouded in darkness, and imperfections and mistakes will no longer be possible with him, as in this life. The apostle continues :—"For now we see through a glass darkly,"—which is a reaffirmation, in the use of a striking figure, of what he had first uttered. In this world, men of even the brightest intellects and the most profound thought, see everything that exists as through a smoked or tarnished glass, "darkly;" that is, imperfectly or obscurely; literally *in an enigma*, or as it stands in the margin, "in a riddle;" "but *then*,"—in the heavenly world,—they shall see "*as face to face ;*" that is, clearly, distinctly, accurately; or, as one expresses it, "without the intervention of any medium that can obscure or distort." And the closing words of the apostle render the whole still more emphatic: "Now I know *in part*, but then shall I know even as also I am known." He was then speaking under the inspiration of the divine spirit, and yet he did not feel to possess the clear, distinct and absolute knowledge of God and Heaven and all things divine in the universe, as he should, when he should stand face to face with eternal realities. THEN HE SHOULD KNOW AS EVEN ALSO HE WAS KNOWN. By which is meant, he should comprehend spirits and spiritual things,—which are the real in God's universe,—in the same manner, with the same clearness and to the same extent, that the angelic hosts and disembodied spirits know and understand; for, as we have seen in these pages, "in the resurrection we shall be "*equal* to the angels of God." "In the future life," says Dr. Channing, "it is reasonable to suppose that our knowledge will embrace what exists in both Heaven and earth. It is not at all inconsistent with what we know of nature, to suppose that those in Heaven, whatever be their abode, may have spiritual senses and organs by which they may discern and comprehend the remote in other spheres, as clearly as we do whatever is near."

Now is it probable or even possible that the human soul will be thus improved and perfected in its powers and capacities, and put in possession of knowledge so vast, and still remain in ignorance of the existence, and, also, the spiritual presence of the dearest objects of its affections when on earth? The parent ignorant of the presence of his child, the child of the parent; the husband ignorant of the presence of his wife, and the wife of her husband? To our mind the thought is most preposterous, that the inhabitants of Heaven shall know everything else but what they most desire to know while on earth, viz. :—the happy and positive existence, the real presence and blessedness of those they most tenderly love. Thank God for the positive declaration: *Then* we shall know the inhabitants of Heaven, with the same certainty that the hosts of the celestial world now know us.

All this is Christian; it is radiant with spiritual beauty and comfort to the mourning soul. Let such as weep because of separations they have experienced from those so dear to them, find consolation in the sweet assurance that they are journeying toward a land of perennial delights, where they shall meet those who have gone before to be welcomed with celestial joy :—

> "Where is the friend, who only yesterday
>   Spoke words of love to me ?
> To-day I call in piteous tones for answer,—
>   No sound comes back to me.
>
> "Where is the darling mother, loved so fondly ?
>   Who, years and years ago,
> Shut eyes so blue, and left our hearts so broken,—
>   Oh! shall I ever know!
>
> "Ah, yes, for every day, makes one the nearer
>   To that bright land so fair,
> Where all our loved ones greet us as we enter,—
>   The lost ones all are there.
>
> "Oh, happy thought! Comes every day the nearer,
>   When I those friends shall see!
> I then shall know why I was left to sorrow,
>   Why they were called to Thee!"

CHAPTER XXII.

Our Knowledge of Those We Love in Heaven.---Objections Considered.

How can Disembodied Spirits be Seen or Known?—Spiritual Forms not only Real but Beautiful.—Methods of Knowing in Heaven not Possessed on Earth.—If we possess Knowledge of each other in Heaven shall we not have Knowledge of the sufferings of those on Earth and in the World of Misery?—And, if so, will not this Knowledge be a source of perpetual sorrow in Heaven?

BUT it is asked by those who object to the sentiments expressed in the preceding chapter:— "How can it be possible that disembodied spirits,—destitute of form and substance, and therefore impalpable and imperceptible to the vision,—can be seen, or their presence known in the immortal life?"

We answer, disembodied spirits are *not* destitute of form or substance. They are represented everywhere in the Scriptures, not only as possessing forms, but most exquisitely beautiful forms,—and, though spiritual in their nature, they must be constituted of elements more real than anything earthly because they are "eternal," while all things earthly are merely "temporal;" and, though so impalpable in their substance as to be imperceptible to the natural vision, to celestial beings their forms are as plainly visible as the grossest substance is to the natural vision.

Our own belief is, that nothing can exceed the beauty or the positive existence of the angels and disembodied spirits, of which Heaven is filled, whose time is spent in the most delightful intercourse and employment, and whose existence is as palpable to each other as our being in these physical forms. And further, we believe that the soul in its disembodied form, when developed through the process of the resurrection, has the power of knowing, or of obtaining knowledge, of which we, in our present sphere, are utterly ignorant. The soul is capable of approximating this condition, even while connected with the gross elements of the physical body. A man in a mesmeric trance, with his eyes bandaged, if a good subject, is capable of describing how many persons are present in a perfectly dark room; in what part of the room they are situated—whether they are seated or standing, how dressed, whether gentlemen or ladies, for what purpose they are there, what is the general character of their minds, the condition of their feelings, etc. All this we have witnessed. How, or by what means or what power, the soul, when in certain conditions, possesses this knowledge, no man can divine; but of the fact itself there can be no question; nor can there be any doubt but the soul arrives at its conclusions without the aid of either of the senses.

Now if all this is true of the soul while connect

ed with the human, physical form, is it not possible —nay, almost certain that it will possess the ability to perform far greater wonders even, when it is divested of its mortal garment and clothed upon with its pure, celestial habiliments? And, if so, why shall we not know of the presence of dear ones in the spirit life by the powers of intuition we shall possess? If the soul possesses this ability in this life it certainly will in the next. Heaven is full of attractions. Even in this world we are attracted by those we love and for whom we feel strong affinity and sympathy. How much more intense will be those attractions in the immortal life. How, then, can the mother be lost to her child, or the child to its mother, in the world of spirits. That woman had the true, Christian faith and was inspired by the maternal instinct, who exclaimed, concerning her babe that had gone :—

> "Thy days, my darling one, were few,
> An angel's morning visit,
> That came and vanished with the dew;—
> 'Twas here—'tis gone;—*where is it?*
> I cannot tell to what sweet dell
> The ange's may have borne thee;
> But this I know, thou canst not go
> Where my heart will fail to find thee."

Some conceive Heaven to be a vast expanse,— very lonely, with only here and there an inhabitant, which renders the thought of death to them very gloomy. Said a dear sister in Christ to us, many years ago, as she lay upon her bed of suffering, expecting every hour to look upon those she loved for the last time on earth:—"Oh, if I could only have some one to go over the river with me! But to go *alone*,—ALL ALONE! It seems so dark, and cold, and lonely! How shall I find my children, my sister, or my dear father and mother? You know how long since mother died; and how shall I know them?"

To hear the poor, anxious soul giving expression to her thoughts in these touching words, affected all in the room to tears, and we tried to comfort her by saying:—

"You will not go alone, dear friend, for Christ will be with you. His promise is, 'Lo, I am with you alway, even to the end of the world.' Look to him in faith and you shall realize he is round and about you affording you strength and peace. The angels a shining throng, with the dear ones gone of whom you speak, may be present and welcome you to the Eden of delights to which you shall be translated, and make all blissful and blessed." And, to our great joy, when breathing her last on the following morning, she was filled with inexpressible delight, at the glimpses of Heaven afforded her. She said that Christ and the holy angels,—her father and mother, her dear children and all her acquaintances, who had passed away, were hovering over her and around her to receive her with open arms and sweet smiles! "Glory! Glory!" she shouted. "Oh, what beauty! what blessedness! what joy!" And in this ecstatic condition of soul, she passed the Jordan of death to the realms of everlasting bliss!

Some call all this delusion, because *they* cannot discern what the soul in this exalted state is made to see and know. *We* believe it to be divine reality! And we bless God for the strength of our faith in it.

Thus do we see how the soul can be known and its presence felt to other spirits in the celestial world, though utterly invisible to our natural senses.

But another, and the principal objection brought against the views presented in the foregoing chapter, is found in the fact, as is said, that a knowledge of the existence in Heaven of those we knew on earth, necessitates the additional knowledge of the world we left,—all its imperfections, sorrows, sufferings and wretchedness, connected with which and enduring which, may be some of our own near relatives and friends. Nay, more,—such knowledge, it is affirmed, also necessitates a knowledge of the sufferings of other dear ones in the world of woe, to which many Christians sincerely believe God has consigned millions upon millions of His sentient creatures. And they ask, how can Heaven prove a place of happiness to any, with a certain knowledge that loved fathers, mothers, brothers, sisters and darling children are suffering in the abyss of woe? They think this impossible; and so do *we*. In Heaven our sympathies will be intensified and our loves enhanced a thousand fold. It is impossible for us even while here on earth sincerely to *believe* in the event described above, and enjoy one moment's peace! How much more impossible will it be for Heaven to prove a place of bliss to us, if, when we arrive there, we shall have *perfect knowledge* of the fact that those absent are in a condition of continual and endless suffering!

To avoid this terrible dilemma, Christians have been driven to the unnatural alternative of declaring that in Heaven we shall have no knowledge of each other; no knowledge of this earth, or of the world of wretchedness; but only knowledge of God, and Christ, and Heaven, and happiness!

All this is but another argument against the possibility of the existence anywhere in the universe of God, of a place created by our ever blessed Father for the endless banishment of His own children. As we have shown in the preceding chapter, we shall have knowledge of each other in the celestial world; and knowledge of God and Christ and of the millions of glorified spirits who shall dwell in the world of bliss. We shall have knowledge of earth, and what is transpiring here,—of the imperfections, sins and sorrows of this life; yet, knowing all this, we shall be happy. God is happy, infinitely happy, and yet His vast mind comprehends the imperfection to which we refer. It is because He also comprehends the means He employs to bring order out of chaos, beauty out of deformity, and perfection out of imperfection. He beholds with unerring certainty all things working toward one grand and glorious result, viz.: the holiness, and perfection, and happiness, and endless bliss of every child of His vast family of created intelligencies. If the sorrow of one single soul of these millions were to be made *endless*, the joys of none could be complete. When we shall arrive in the world of perfection and no longer "see as through a glass *darkly*," but as "face to face," and "know as also we are known," we shall comprehend, as do the angels, what now seems so mysterious to us,—all will be found to belong to one harmonious whole, whose body nature is and God the soul, and we shall rest in the delightful assurance that Christ must reign until all things are subdued unto him, and God become "all in all!"

Not in a long time have we seen anything more Christian and more in harmony with our own thought on the subject embraced in the above objection, than the following brief extract from the pen of Rev. Dr. Chauning. He says:—

"To say that a knowledge of the misery of earth will make us miserable in Heaven, is a reproach to Heaven and the good. It supposes that the happiness of that world is founded in ignorance; that it is the happiness of the blind man, who, were he to open his eyes on what exists around him, would be filled with horror. It makes Heaven an elysium, whose inhabitants perpetuate their joy by shutting themselves up in narrow bounds and hiding themselves from the pains of their fellow creatures. But the good from their very natures cannot be thus confined. Heaven would be a prison, did it cut them off from sympathy with the suffering. Their benevolence is too pure, too divine to shrink from the sight of evil. Let me add, that this declaration casts reproach on God, too. It supposes that there are regions of His universe which must be kept out of sight, because if seen they would blight the happiness of the humane and virtuous. But this cannot be! There are no such regions,—no secret places of woe which these pure spirits must not penetrate. There is impiety in the thought. The very existence of such places would preclude the possibility of Heaven as a place of bliss to any in the universe."

From all we have said, the reader will see our reasons for believing that in Heaven we shall not only know and comprehend each other better than in our earth life, but our souls will be quickened and perfected, and our knowledge of all created things,—even the far off splendors of the universe, —will be enhanced *ad infinitum*; all of which will add ten thousand fold to our means of enjoyment. All this is taught in God's precious Word and is no more than the goodness and power of our dear Father in Heaven would inspire us to anticipate, thanks to His glorious name!

"Shall We Know the Loved Ones There?"

And shall we know the dear ones there,
   In you bright world of love and bliss,
When, on the wings of ambient air,
   Our spirits soar away from this?
Or must we feel the ceaseless pain
   Of absence in that glorious sphere,
And search through Heaven's bright hosts in vain
   The sainted forms we've cherished here?

Will not their hearts demand us there,—
   Those hearts, whose fondest throbs were given
To us on earth, whose every prayer
   Petitioned for our ties in Heaven?
Whose love outlived the stormy past,
   And closer twined around us here,
And deeper grew until the last,—
   Say, will they not demand us there?

Will they not wander lonely o'er
   Those fields of light and life above,
If spirits they have loved of yore
   Respond not to the call of love?
And though the glory of the skies,
   And seraph's glittering crowns they wear,
Though Heaven's full radiance greet their eyes,
   Still, will they not demand us there:

It must be so; for Heaven is home,
   Where severed spirits reunite;
And from the basement to its dome,
   Are altars sacred to the rite;
And joy doth strike her golden strings,
   And holier seems that home of bliss,
As some reft heart from earth upsprings
   To meet in that, the loved of this.

CHAPTER XXIII.

Heaven a Home of Blessedness for All.

The Grand Consummation of the Gospel.—Why should we fear the Change called Death?—Christ and Death at the Gate of Nain.—Dr. Priestly and the Rev. John Murray when dying.—A Home in Heaven for All.

AND so then we come to the grand consummation, declared in the divine Word, that Heaven is to be the ultimate Home of all God's great family. No one shall be absent. Blessed thought! "In my Father's house there are *many* mansions." Oh, yes, thanks to God, mansions *enough* for all;—and every one of them beautiful beyond conception, with all their perfected appointments of health and comfort and spiritual culture! How charming the conception of a grand, old homestead full of cheer, to which the children and grandchildren and great grandchildren can return to greet once more the dear ones of life, and enjoy a blissful reunion in a home of blessedness and abundance! But how much more beautiful our Home in Heaven, where we shall be lifted above the mists and clouds of this world into the full blaze of divine light, life and love, where there shall be no more sin, or sorrow, or death, or suffering;—no more wanderings from our Father's house, or weariness, or want, or parting, or sighing, or tears. This is what the Christian faith in its fullness and purity teaches. And further, that the family in Heaven shall be unbroken. No link shall be absent from the golden chain. In our earthly homes, some are absent. The vacant chair occupies every dwelling. But in Heaven every member shall be there. Why, then, should we fear the change we call death, when it only releases from the toils and sufferings and disappointments of this life, which shall be succeeded by love that is immortal and peace that shall never end. Why should we weep over the remains of those so precious to us, when these beautiful truths, radiant with celestial life, are felt in our souls, and shine into and all through the tomb, making it bright and beautiful with the sweetest hope. The dear ones gone are still living. We shall go to them. Do you not remember how, just outside of the gate of the city of Nain, the blessed Jesus met Death, followed by a weeping mother, and how he showed the gathering throng his instant and complete power over the monster? "Young man, I say unto thee, arise!" That was enough. Death dropped. He was conquered. That poor woman never expected to look into the eyes of her son, or listen to his sweet voice, or feel his soft kiss upon her cheek again. See how her tears start and her heart throbs! "O, my son! my son!" "HE DELIVERED HIM TO HIS MOTHER!" Dear reader, do you hear *that*?

Oh, ye troubled souls; ye, who have lived to see every prospect blasted; every friend desert you; all your dear ones taken from you! Do you hear that? They shall all be delivered to you again, and in a Home that shall never, never end!

What a blessed heritage of peace and strength in this hope. How many thousands have been consoled by it in the last moments of their existence. Said the Rev. Dr. Priestly to his sorrowing wife and weeping children, as he was breathing his last: "Weep not, my darlings. I go to heavenly joys, to greet again those I loved on earth in mansions of bliss, where we all shall meet in holy communion by and by." And, exclaimed the Rev. John Murray, when about to die: "I feel as if I were voyaging to my native shores, where my loved friends, and health, and wealth, and divine happiness await me. Oh, let propitious gales waft me onward, for I pant to be there!" It is a source of great joy to meet with those we love, after long absence, in this world;—for the mariner to return to his home when years of danger and peril have passed, and fold to his heart the loved members of his family and receive their salutations of welcome and expressions of joy. But how much more blessed the thought of the reunion in Heaven of all God's great family, purified from the pollution of sin, elevated to divine realities, with a divine nature, only to love and serve God and one another, forever and ever. When a dear child of King David was taken from his embrace, he said: "While the child was yet alive, I fasted and wept; for I said, who can tell whether God will be gracious to me that the child may live. But now he is dead, wherefore should I fast? Can I bring him back again? I SHALL GO TO HIM, but he will not return to me." Blessed thought. We shall go to them. No matter how poor, or forlorn, or forsaken is our condition in this life, we shall go to them, for we

ALL HAVE A HOME IN HEAVEN.

"A Home in Heaven! What a joyful thought
As the poor man toils in his weary lot;
The heart oppressed, and with anguish driven,
From his Home below, to his Home in Heaven.

"A Home in Heaven, when our pleasures fade,
And our Wealth and Fame in the dust are laid;
And Strength decays, and our Health is riven,
We are happy still, if we think on Heaven.

"A Home in Heaven, when the faint heart bleeds
By the spirit's stroke for its evil deeds;
Oh, then what bliss in that heart forgiven,
Does the hope inspire of a Home in Heaven!

"A Home in Heaven, when our friends are fled
To the cheerless gloom of the mouldering dead;
We wait in Hope on the promise given;
We will meet up there in our Home in Heaven!

"A Home in Heaven! O that glorious Home,
And the spirit joined with the bride say "come;"
Come seek his face, and your sins forgiven,
Rejoice in Hope of your Home in Heaven!"

CHAPTER XXIV.

Letter of Condolence from Benjamin Franklin.

The Present Life Transient.—The Future Real.—The Benevolence of God plainly Exhibited in the Change called Death.—We must Surrender our Mortal Bodies for the Immortal.—Beautiful, Comforting Thought.

THE following remarkable letter of condolence was written by BENJAMIN FRANKLIN,—the "Sage, Philosopher and Statesman,"—to his daughter on the death of his brother, John Franklin, one hundred and twenty years ago. It is very simple, yet wonderfully profound and full of beautiful, Christian thought. Every word is a pearl set in gold. We give it in this place because its ideas are so Christian, so entirely in harmony with the doctrine taught in this book and so full of comfort and consolation to the bereaved and those about to die. It was not designed by its author for the public eye, yet, neither Socrates, nor Solomon, nor Confucius ever produced expressions so pregnant with sweet and sublime thought to comfort and bless, as none of them wrote from the inspiration of a Christian Hope :—

Philadelphia, Feb. 12, 1756.

DEAR CHILD :—I condole with you. We have lost a most dear and valuable relative, but it is the will of God and Nature that these mortal bodies be laid aside when the soul is to enter into real life. Existence here on earth is hardly to be called life. 'Tis rather an embryo state—a preparation to living. A man is not completely born until he is dead. Why, then, should we grieve that a new child is born among the immortals—a new member added to their society?

We are spirits. That bodies should be lent to us while they can afford us pleasure, assist us in acquiring knowledge, or in doing good to our fellow-creatures, is a kind and benevolent act of God. When they become unfit for their purposes, and afford us pain instead of pleasure, instead of an aid become an encumbrance, and answer none of the intentions for which they were given, it is equally kind and benevolent that a way is provided by which we may get rid of them. That way is death.

We ourselves, prudently in some cases, choose a partial death. A mangled, painful limb, which cannot be restored, we willingly cut off. He that plucks out a tooth parts with it freely, since the pain goes with it, and he that quits the whole body parts with all the pains and possibility of pains and diseases it was liable to or capable of making him suffer.

Our friend and we are invited abroad on a party of pleasure that is to last forever. His chair* was first ready and he has gone before us. We could not conveniently all start together; and why should you and I be aggrieved at this, since we are soon to follow, and we know where to find him?

Adieu, my dear, good child, and believe that I shall be, in every state, your affectionate papa,

BENJ. FRANKLIN.

---

* Alluding to the sedan chair then in fashion in which to ride out.

When the Mists have Rolled Away We Shall Know as We are Known.

When the mists have rolled in splendor
  From the beauty of the hills,
And the sunshine, warm and tender,
  Falls in kisses on the rills,
We may read love's shining letter
  In the rainbow of the spray;
We shall know each other better
  When the mists have rolled away.

  We shall know as we are known,
    Never more to walk alone,
  In the dawning of the morning,
    When the mists have cleared away.

If we err in human blindness,
  And forget that we are dust;
If we miss the law of kindness
  When we struggle to be just,
Snowy wings of peace shall cover
  All the anguish of to-day,
When the weary watch is over,
  And the mists have cleared away.

When the silver mist has veiled us
  From the faces of our own,
Oft we deem their love has failed us,
  And we tread our path alone;
We should see them near and truly,
  We should trust them day by day,
Neither love nor blame unduly,
  If the mists were cleared away.

When the mists have ris'n above us,
  As our Father knows His own,
Face to face with those who love us,
  We shall know as we are known.
Love, beyond the orient meadows,
  Floats the golden fringe of day;
Heart to heart we'll bide the shadows
  Till the mists have cleared away.

My Little Boy in Heaven.*

My child,—my little boy,—was lying dead.
    They had covered the body with flowers,
And it lay there, so cold and so silent,—
    In that sorrowful home of ours.

Only one sunrise and sunset
    Had illumined the world with their flames,
Since our beautiful, mischievous darling
    Had romped with his mates at their games.

Just the night before last he was nestling
    Here in my arms after dark,
And talking his sweet, wise nonsense;—
    I can hear it now, almost:—Hark!

And his golden hair, uncurled and tangled,
    Was brushing my bosom, so;—
And his cheeks were flushed with excitement,—
    And, now,—they're as white as the snow.

Oh!—I cannot, I cannot, my darling,
    Let you slip from my holding just yet;
The angels must sing on without you;
    Come back to your mother's arms, pet.

But he came not,—he would not, he could not;—
    And my brain in the pressure grew wild,
And I traversed the great house in madness,
    Mournfully calling my child.

I avoided the darkened parlors,
    Where the little form lay in state,—
For they made it all real to me,
    And I was denying fate.

But when the shadows of twilight
    Were over the whole world thrown,
I stole back again to the casket,—
    For I could not leave him alone.

And I took him out into my bosom,
    And the flowers fell over the floor,
And I cuddled, and petted, and kissed him,
    And feigned he was mine once more.

---

* Written for this work by Miss Nettie Waltze.

And the shadows grew denser around us,—
   And closer I nestled the child,
Till out of the edge of the heavens,
   A joyous young moon rose and smiled.

And there came a great calm with the moonrise,
   For the worlds of the spirits near swung;
And I saw their white raiment and shining,
   And I heard the sweet songs that they sung.

And the boy I had lost was among them,—
   Those wonderful, glittering throngs!—
And his voice with the olden musical
   Cadences blent with their songs.

Beautiful, I had named him,
   When I called him, and thought him mine,
But ah!—that mortal loveliness
   Was faint to the grace divine

That now upon form and feature
   Had set an immortal seal;
As, alone, your perfect radiances
   O Heaven, could my boy reveal!

I knew not the real charm of my seraph
   Till God set him up there in the light;
And then, in a flood of surprises,
   They poured their full force on my sight.

And I felt that not e'en the divineness
   Of having him back for my own,
Would compensate the slightest marring
   Of the joy in his whole face that shone.

He was happy,—and I would be happy
   In thinking of his changeless joy,
Oh! our Father was so good to give me
   One glimpse of my glorified boy!

And I laid down with many caresses,
   The dear, little body to rest,
And feeling so sure in my sorrow,
   That, whatever the pain,—it was best.

And so, evermore, I'm rejoicing,—
   Howsoe'er long life's grief, or how wild,—
Because I've a home in the heavens,
   Where God will restore me my child.

And no earthly home rapture could bring me
Such exquisite fervors of joy,
As to live thus, unselfish and patient,
Fully blest in the bliss of my boy!

To Alice Among the Angels.*

Beautiful spirit!—dwelling in light,
  And crowned with immortal roses,
We, in the chill of our earthly night
'Mid the blossoms that droop, and the buds that blight,
Look yearningly up to your splendid height,
  Where eternal calm reposes;
And plead to gaze into your pure, still face,
  To hold for a moment your living hands,
To *know* all your life in its varying grace,
  In the depths of those mystical lands,
With their fresh, bright bloom,
    And their singing birds,
      Their rythmical flow
    Of golden words,
    That only the angels know.
Our wings are hidden, but yours are grown,
  And have carried you out of our reach,
We cannot follow where you have flown
  Save by our human speech.
We breathe soft whispers into the air,
And we think they are heard by the angels there!
O Alice, dear Alice, sweet Alice,—we know
You have not forgotten us here below;
Be with us often, and help us to climb
From our low, sad place, to your height sublime.

---

* Written for this work by Miss Nettie Waltae.

The Aged.—"Only Waiting."

A very aged Christian, who was so poor as to be in an almshouse, was asked what he was doing now. He replied, "Only waiting."

Only waiting till the shadows
 Are a little longer grown;
Only waiting till the glimmer
 Of the day's last beam is flown;
Till the night of earth is faded
 From the heart once full of day;
Till the stars of Heaven are breaking
 Through the twilight soft and gray.

Only waiting till the reapers
 Have the last sheaf gathered home;
For the summer-time is faded,
 And the autumn winds have come.
Quickly, reapers, gather quickly
 The last ripe hours of my heart,
For the bloom of life is withered,
 And I hasten to depart.

Only waiting till the angels
 Open wide the mystic gate,
At whose feet I long have lingered,
 Weary, poor, and desolate.
Even now I hear the footsteps,
 And their voices, far away;
If they call me, I am waiting,
 Only waiting to obey.

Only waiting till the shadows
 Are a little longer grown;
Only waiting till the glimmer
 Of the day's last beam is flown;
Then from out the gathered darkness
 Holy, deathless stars shall rise,
By whose light my soul shall gladly
 Tread its pathway to the skies.

www.ingramcontent.com/pod-product-compliance
Lightning Source LLC
Chambersburg PA
CBHW031950230426
43672CB00010B/2109